L. Todière

The Last Cæsars of Byzantium

L. Todière

The Last Cæsars of Byzantium

ISBN/EAN: 9783337101664

Printed in Europe, USA, Canada, Australia, Japan

Cover: Foto ©ninafisch / pixelio.de

More available books at **www.hansebooks.com**

THE LAST CÆSARS

OF

BYZANTIUM.

TRANSLATED FROM THE FRENCH

L. TODIERE.

PHILADELPHIA:
H. L. KILNER & CO.,
Publishers.

COPYRIGHT, 1891,
BY
H. L. KILNER & CO.

AUTHOR'S PREFACE.

I OFFER to the public a volume which may derive interest from the present attitude of Russia and Turkey in regard to each other, and from the great Russian-Turkish question which now claims the attention of every European Government. It contains a simple narrative of the events which agitated the Byzantine empire, from the accession of the Palæologi to the conquest of Greece by the Ottomans. I have endeavored to trace, together with the rapid progress of the Turks, the decline of the Greeks, whilst province after province is subjugated, and one by one cities are snatched from their grasp, until at last the fall of the capital dealt the fatal blow to that power which had ruled for so many centuries.

For the proper treatment of a subject so vast in its details, I have been obliged to consult various authors and examine numerous documents. I have not narrated any important fact without referring to the authority whence it was derived. Justice requires me to mention the names of some historians from whose works I have drawn so largely, that I may name them my fellow-laborers. Such are John Cantacuzenus, who shared the throne with John V. Palæologus, and who was an esteemed writer, author of a *History of the Empire of the East* from 1320 to 1357; Michael Ducas, a descendant of the imperial family of Ducas, and living at the time of the taking of Constantinople by Mahomet II., who has left us a *History of the Empire of the East* from John Cantacuzenus to the conquest of the Empire, in a work remarkable for its truth and justice; and I may add to these the names of Laonicus Chalcondyle, of Athens, and of George Phranza or Phrantzes, Governor of Morea in 1446, from whose pen we have a *Chronicle of Constantinople* from 1259 to 1477. Having employed the most scrupulous care in collecting reliable accounts of the events connected with the period of which I write, I trust that my work may be favorably received.

TABLE OF CONTENTS.

PAGE

CHAPTER I.
RETURN OF THE GREEKS TO CONSTANTINOPLE—THE EMPEROR MICHAEL PALÆOLOGUS 7

CHAPTER II.
CIVIL DISCORD—PROGRESS OF THE OTTOMANS 35

CHAPTER III.
BAJAZET AND TAMERLANE 64

CHAPTER IV.
PEACE IN THE EMPIRE—MANUEL OPPOSES MUSTAPHA TO THE SULTAN AMURAT II. 98

CHAPTER V.
PROGRESS OF THE OTTOMANS—UNION OF THE CHURCHES 126

CHAPTER VI.
HUNNIADES AND SCANDERBEG 151

CHAPTER VII.

PREPARATIONS FOR THE SIEGE OF CONSTANTINOPLE—
CONSTERNATION OF THE GREEKS 177

CHAPTER VIII.

SIEGE AND FALL OF CONSTANTINOPLE—DESTRUCTION
OF THE EMPIRE OF THE EAST 201

CHAPTER IX.

MAHOMET AT CONSTANTINOPLE—CONQUEST OF PELO-
PONNESUS—END OF THE DYNASTY OF THE PALÆO-
LOGI 234

THE LAST CÆSARS OF BYZANTIUM.

CHAPTER I.

RETURN OF THE GREEKS TO CONSTANTINOPLE—
THE EMPEROR MICHAEL PALÆOLOGUS.

Family and character of Michael Palæologus—Disgrace and death of Muzalon—Michael Palæologus named Despot, then Emperor—Embassy of Baldwin to Palæologus—The Emperor fails in his attack upon Constantinople—The Cæsar Strategopulus marches towards the City—Taking of Constantinople—Flight of the Latins—Entrance of Michael into the City—Venetians, Pisans and Genoese established at Constantinople—Honor accorded to Stratagopulus—Michael Palæologus puts out the eyes of John Lascaris—Grief of the Patriarch Arsenius—He excommunicates the Emperor—Insurrection of the Mountaineers of Nicæa—Deposition and exile of Arsenius—Abdication of his successor—The monk Joseph elected Patriarch—Absolution of the Emperor—Condition of the provinces of the East—Expedition against the Duke of Patras—Andronicus associated in the Empire—Union of Palæologus with the Latin Church—The Greeks persecuted—Union dissolved—League against the Emperor—Death of Michael Palæologus—Andronicus II. Emperor—Roger de Flor—Exploits of the Catalans—Revolt of Andronicus the Younger.

As early as the middle of the eleventh century, the noble family of the Palæologi appears with honor in the history of Constantinople. If the father of the Comneni was able to place upon his brow the crown of the Cæsars, he was indebted for it to George Palæologus, whose descendants continued to command armies, to preside over councils of state, and to exercise a vast authority. Their alliance was sought by the imperial family, and if the law of female succession had been rigorously observed, the wife of Theodore Lascaris would have made way for the elder sister, the mother of that Michael Palæologus, who afterwards elevated his family to the throne. To noble birth, Michael Palæologus united brilliant qualities. Brave, accomplished, generous, eloquent, affable in his manners and conversation, he won all hearts. But the affection of the people and the army deprived him of favor at Court, and this prince thrice escaped the dangers to which he was exposed by the imprudence of his followers. The Emperor Theodore Lascaris, one of those fugitive Greeks who had replaced and maintained the Roman standard on the walls of Nicæa in Bithynia, in spite of the efforts of the Latins, then masters of Constantinople, had on his death-bed recommended his son John, six years of age, to Palæologus, whose talents and influence he well knew (1259). At the same time he appointed as his guardian, with absolute control, George Muzalon, his chief favorite, associating, however, with him the Patriarch of Nicæa, Arsenius.

The hatred entertained by the Greeks towards Muzalon had been expressed during the life of the Emperor, but it burst forth in undisguised fury after his death. Unable to cope openly with his enemies, the tutor endeavored to disarm their malice by gentleness; he convened at the palace an assembly consisting of the high nobility, the magistracy, the most distinguished officers of the army, and presented himself before them clothed in the insignia of his various dignities. In a crafty discourse, he offered aloud from the throne an explanation of his conduct, expressing his willingness to renounce the regency if they should judge his abdication conducive to the public good. The destruction of Muzalon had been determined, but his enemies considered that the favorable moment had not yet arrived; they overwhelmed his pretended modesty with protestations of esteem and fidelity, and his most implacable enemies were apparently the most eager to renew their oath of obedience. Among these, Michael Palæologus, who even in boyhood had been elevated to the office of Constable or of Commandant of the mercenary chiefs, urgently implored the guardian and savior of the Romans not to renounce the guardianship of the young Emperor. Never had the Greeks been so perfidious, and the regent was soon the dupe of his credulity and ambition. On the ninth day after the death of Lascaris, the solemnity of his obsequies was celebrated according to custom, in the cathedral of Magnesia, a city of Asia. In the midst of the ceremonies, the guards rushed into the church, uttering horrible imprecations, and massacred, at the foot of the altar, Muzalon, his brothers, and all their partisans. Under these circumstances, Michael conducted himself in such a manner as to derive all the advantage of the massacre without participating in the crime, or, at least, without suffering the odium attaching to it. Claiming no honors, he trusted to the effect of his liberality, the more valued from the diminution of his fortune. The great lords having assembled to elect a regent, offered him the title of Grand Duke, and Arsenius left in his hands all executive authority.

From that moment the ambitious Palæologus regarded his dignity only as a stepping stone by which the more easily to ascend the throne to which he aspired. The ascendency of his genius either won over or divided the factions of the nobles. John Ducas-Vataces, the predecessor of Theodore Lascaris, had deposited immense treasures in a fortress situated on the banks of the Hermus, under the guard of the faithful Varangians, foreign troops of Norman descent. The Constable had acquired so great an influence over these men, that he obtained possession of the treasure without opposition, and made use of it to corrupt the guards. To diminish the amount of taxes, a cause of continual discontent among the people, to forbid the ordeal by fire and judicial combats, to provide for the maintenance of the widows and children of the veteran soldiers, were among the first acts of the new regent. Knowing the influence of the clergy, he strove to secure the adhesion of this powerful order. Secret liberalities seduced all the schismatical prelates, and even the incorruptible Patriarch was gained by homage which flattered his vanity. At the same time, his emissaries mingling among the people, intimated that the tender age of the emperor demanded an associate, one in the prime of life, who united experience to superior talents. On his side, Palæologus hinted that a precarious authority should not be conferred upon him who was to hold the reins of government.

These pretensions aroused the whole city of Magnesia, whither the Court had been removed. The advantages of an elective monarchy were freely discussed, and the Grand Duke increased the number of his partisans by promises of a just administration of the laws and the reformation of all abuses. If his assertions could be relied upon, he impatiently awaited the moment when the young emperor would be able to dispense with his services, and he himself could return to the peaceful obscurity of private life. His dexterous management silenced his opponents; and the title and prerogatives of *despot* were conferred upon him. He thus enjoyed all the honors of the purple and the second rank in the empire. It was next decreed that Michael Palæologus should be crowned emperor jointly with John Lascaris. The clergy, who had been convinced of the necessity of his election by the money of the despot, considered that they sufficiently fulfilled their duty towards the young son of Theodore, by exacting of his colleague an oath to resign his authority as soon as Lascaris should attain his majority. The prelates assured Palæologus that far from perjuring himself by accepting the crown, he would merit an immortal crown by so generously sacrificing his own repose to the public good. He received the imperial diadem in the cathedral of Nicæa, from the patriarch Arsenius, who had, however, only with extreme repugnance abandoned the interests of his pupil. The grateful Palæologus liberally dispensed civil and military employments to his partisans, loaded with honors the members of his family, and bestowed the title of Cæsar upon the aged Alexis Strategopulus (1260).

The new emperor strove to strengthen his power by gaining the love of his subjects. He appeared frequently in public, addressed the people, and heightened the effect of his eloquence by gifts of money. He went to Nympha, the usual residence of the emperors after they had lost Constantinople. Hoping to recover by negotiation, at least, some provinces or cities, the emperor Baldwin sent ambassadors to him requesting of him the cession of Thessalonica. Palæologus replied with insulting raillery that he could not honorably abandon a city which held the remains of his father. "Grant us the city of Serres," said the deputies. "It was there," answered Palæologus, "that I fought my first battle." To their demand for Boliva, the Greek returned a refusal upon the plea that it was an admirable hunting ground. The deputies still insisting, asked: "What then, will you give us?" "Nothing; but if you desire peace you must pay me as an annual tribute the proceeds of the taxes of Constantinople. The refusal of your master will be the signal of war. I am not deficient in military experience, and for success I rely upon God and my sword."

Michael Palæologus was, in reality, meditating no less a project than the expulsion of the Latins from Byzantium. The present moment appeared most favorable to him; the distress of the city was at its height. After having visited all the fortresses of Thrace, and augmented their garrisons, he placed himself at the head of an army, crossed the Hellespont, marched towards the capital, obtained possession of the greater part of the suburbs, and so restricted the Latin empire, that it scarcely extended beyond the walls of Constantinople. An attack upon Galata proved unsuccessful; he relied upon the concurrence of a perfidious nobleman, who was either unable or unwilling to open the gates. Every assault was repulsed, and his great losses forced him to withdraw into Asia.

The following spring, the Cæsar Alexis Strategopulus, his favorite general, crossed the Hellespont with eight hundred knights and a few hundred foot soldiers, in order to watch the movements of the Bulgarians. His instructions directed him to approach Constantinople, to examine carefully the condition of the city, to take advantage of any opportunity which might present, but not to venture upon a doubtful enterprise. The Greeks scattered throughout the adjoining country hastened eagerly to the camp of the Cæsar, whose army soon numbered twenty-five thousand men. These volunteers well knew the deplorable condition of the Latins, which had daily come under their observation. They assured the old general that if he would attack the capital, it must necessarily fall into his power; that the time was favorable, for there remained within the city only women and children. An imprudent young officer, recently nominated governor of the colony of Venice, had gone out with thirty galleys and the élite of the Latin knights upon an expedition against the city of Daphnusia, situated on the Black sea, a short distance from Byzantium.

Notwithstanding the prohibition of the emperor, the Cæsar, after a few moments' hesitation, resolved to risk the attack, and took every precaution necessary to ensure success. Leaving the body of the army at a certain distance, in order to second him as circumstances might require, he advanced under cover of the darkness, with a detachment of picked men. He introduced into a subterranean passage which had been made known to him by a Greek deserter, about fifty determined men, for the purpose of breaking open the Golden Gate, which had been closed many years, whilst others were ordered to scale in silence the wall where its height was the least. A priest among the assailants was the first to cry out: "Victory and long life to Michael and John, the august emperors of the Romans!" This was the signal agreed upon. The soldiers stationed near the ramparts repeated the acclamation, and rushed toward the gate, which was thrown open to them. In the meantime Strategopulus had sent orders to the remaining troops to advance.

Day was just dawning when the auxiliary troops, consisting of Comans, dispersed in every direction. The Cæsar had scarcely passed the Golden Gate when he trembled at his rashness; fully aware by long experience of the dangers incurred by a victorious army in their capture of a city, he paused, he deliberated. But, encouraged by the numerous volunteers who flocked to his standard, and who urged that a retreat would be more difficult and disastrous than an attack, he advanced, leading his troops in order of battle. The alarm was given, and the soldiers fell upon all whom they found armed, massacred them and commenced to pillage the city. In the midst of the tumult, the Greeks of Constantinople, who were attached to their former masters, and the Genoese merchants, considering the alliance recently made between their republic and Michael Palæologus, took a decided stand. The men rushed to arms, and the people of the city soon shouted with the soldiers of the fortunate Alexis: "Victory and long life to the emperors Michael and John!"

Awakened by the cries, Baldwin II. rushed from his palace; but he did not draw his sword, he only thought of seeking safety by flight. He ran to the shore, dropping on the way his crown, his sword, and all the insignia of royalty. Some Greek soldiers collected these precious spoils and carried them to their generals, who, suspending them on the point of a lance, exhibited them as a trophy to the troops, inciting them thus to deeds of valor and crushing the hopes of the Latins. Fortunately the fleet, having returned from its fruitless expedition against Daphnusia, was entering the Bosphorus.

Constantinople was irrevocably lost; the Latin emperor and the principal families embarked therefore on the Venetian galleys in the midst of the inhuman railleries of the conquerors. Baldwin, who of all his possessions carried with him only the empty title of emperor, sailed to the island of Negroponte and thence crossed into Italy, where the Pope received him with the compassion due so great a misfortune. It was in this manner that the Greeks recovered Byzantium, 25 July, 1261, fifty-seven years after having been driven from it.

Michael Palæologus was residing in the palace at Nymphea, near Smyrna, when an obscure and unknown man, allured by the hope of a recompense, carried him the news of the capture of Constantinople. As the messenger produced no letter from the victorious general, the emperor placed no reliance upon his assertion. He could not be persuaded that Strategopulus, who had left with only eight hundred men, could so easily have made himself master of an immense city in which he, the preceding year, had been unable to obtain a foothold with a large army. He ordered the man to be detained in prison, promising him a handsome reward if he spoke the truth, but death if he lied. After a few hours of agitation, alternating between fear and hope, the emperor was convinced by the arrival of couriers from Alexis, bringing the trophies of victory, the imperial ornaments abandoned by Baldwin in his precipitate flight. Then he assembled the prelates, nobles and senators, and with them returned thanks to the Supreme Author of all success. This event diffused the greatest joy throughout the country. Theodore Torinice, an old man of great good sense, being on his death-bed, learning the cause of the universal rejoicing, not sharing the sentiment of all around him, began to weep. "What!" exclaimed his friends, "we have recovered our country, and you shed tears?" "Alas!" replied the old man, who seemed with prophetic eye to see the future, "the empire is now doomed to pillage. Michael is master of Constantinople: he will fix his residence in that voluptuous city; he will be followed by our warriors who have so long been accustomed to combat the Turks. They will live at court, they will become corrupted by an effeminate life. The Turks will descend from their mountains, they will pass into Europe, they will ultimately obtain possession of Constantinople and the empire."

Twenty days after the expulsion of the Latins, Michael entered Constantinople in triumph, accompanied by his wife, his son, still a child, and by all the lords of his court. At his approach, the Golden Gate was thrown open, the emperor alighted from his horse, and caused to be carried before him a miraculous image of the Blessed Virgin, surnamed the Guide, in order that the Mother, the Patroness and Guardian of the city, might seem herself to conduct him to the temple of her Son, the cathedral of St. Sophia. Palæologus found his capital in a most ruined condition. His first care was to repair it; he invited the families of the old inhabitants who were scattered throughout the empire to return; he restored to the nobles the palaces of their ancestors; all who presented properly attested claims were allowed to take possession of their property.

Three commercial nations, the Venetians, the Pisans, and the Genoese, had manufactories at Constantinople. Instead of banishing them, he received their oath of fidelity, encouraged them, confirmed their privileges, and permitted them to preserve their own magistrates. In order to prevent any disorder, the emperor transferred the Genoese, who were the most numerous and who deserved well from the Greeks, to the faubourg of Galata, after having destroyed the fortifications; the Venetians and Pisans continued to occupy their separate quarters.

Michael Palæologus had conquered but a small portion of that vast domain called the Greek Empire of the East, which the great Theodosius had transmitted to his son Arcadius. Egypt and Syria now belonged to the Mamelukes; the empire of Trebizonde, founded by the grandsons of Andronicus on the southern coast of the Euxine sea, remained independent. The Turkish sultany of Iconium extended over the greater part of Asia Minor, and of all its ancient possessions the empire retained in Asia only Paphlagonia, Bithynia, Mysia, Phrygia, Caria, and a part of Cilicia. On the continent of Europe, the Danube and the gorges of the Hermus bounded on the north and south the new kingdom of the Bulgarians. Servia, founded in the time of Heraclius, bearing in the northeast the name of Rascia, occupied, like the Bulgarians, a portion of the right bank of the Danube, and extended also along the shore of the Adriatic from Ragusa to Scutari, and south as far as the mountains of Macedonia. The principalities founded by the chiefs of the fourth crusade in the centre and south of Greece still subsisted; the Venetians possessed the islands, with Modon and Coron in the Morea; Thebes, Athens, Corinth, Patras and Pylos, composed the independent principality of Achaia; that of Epirus was formed of Etolia, Arcania, Epirus, and a part of Thessaly. The new emperor had acquired possession only of the southeast coast of Peloponnesus.

Whilst Michael was striving to restore Constantinople to its ancient splendor, he was also taking steps to procure the return of the patriarch Arsenius, who, foreseeing the sad fate awaiting the legitimate prince, had abandoned the care of his flock and retired into solitude. Another patriarch, Nicephorus, Bishop of Ephesus, had been installed with great honors in the see of Nicæa, and this new election caused a schism in the Greek Church. As by the death of Nicephorus the patriarchal see had become vacant, the emperor consulted the bishops who had come from distant places to attend his entry into the capital, and after long deliberation he resolved to recall Arsenius. The latter, wearied of his voluntary exile, could not resist the desire to revisit his native land, and consented to resume his former dignity. He, therefore, returned to Constantinople, and the emperor, accompanied by the synod, the principal officers of his court, and a large concourse of people, conducted the prelate to St. Sophia. There taking the patriarch by the hand, he said: "Here is the chair of which you have too long deprived yourself: enjoy it now for the sake of the salvation of the flock confided to your care." At the same time he put him in possession of all the property belonging to the patriarchate.

Hitherto Michael had been too much engrossed by other cares to bestow upon Strategopulus the recompense of his brilliant conquest. He esteemed none he could bestow equal to the service rendered him by the General; he imagined new ways of expressing his gratitude, and decreed him sovereign honors. Strategopulus, clothed in the decorations of a Cæsar, was drawn through the streets in a magnificent chariot, followed by the applause of the Greeks intoxicated with joy. His brow was surmounted by a jewelled crown similar to the emperor's, and he was granted the privilege of wearing it the rest of his life. For the space of one year his name was to be joined to that of the emperor in all expeditions, acclamations, and public prayers.

They next celebrated the return of the Greeks to Constantinople as though it were the establishment of a new empire, and Palæologus desired to repeat in the cathedral of St. Sophia the ceremony of his coronation. Dazzled by the splendors of the restoration and the deference paid him by the ambitious colleague of John Lascaris, the patriarch allowed himself to be persuaded that this second coronation injured in no manner the rights of his legitimate sovereign, and again he placed the diadem upon the brow of Palæologus. The designs of the emperor, slowly and artfully laid, were now approaching maturity. He had by degrees and imperceptibly deprived Lascaris of all honors, he had omitted his name in the acts of the government, and had finally withdrawn from the august child all the support he might have found in his family. Of his five older sisters, two had already been given in marriage to foreign princes. For the three others he selected noblemen of the most distinguished birth, but too weak to give him cause to dread their vengeance. Having thus deprived the young prince of all consideration in the government and of the protection of his relatives, he determined to secure to himself the possession of the throne, by ordering his eyes to be put out. Instead of tearing them out, the ministers of this barbarous command destroyed the optic nerve by means of the reflection of rays from a metal plate heated to redness. John Lascaris was then sent under a strong guard to the castle of Dacybiza, where he languished in obscurity for many years.

Intimidated by the cruelty of the hypocritical

usurper, his degraded courtiers either applauded his act or refrained from any expression of indignation. Not so with the patriarch Arsenius, always inaccessible to the temptations of fear or hope. Upon learning the sad fate of his pupil, he abandoned himself to the deepest despair. Compassion and anger roused all the powers of his soul; he beat his breast, he cried aloud, he called upon the elements to avenge the horrid crime, he tore out his hair and beard, exclaiming: "O sun, tremble! O earth, lament! detest this atrocious deed, this unmerciful ferocity!" He resolved to have recourse to spiritual arms, and in a synod of bishops, animated by his example, he excommunicated the emperor and all his accomplices (1262), And yet in the midst of his just indignation he pronounced the sentence with some mitigation in the formula, omitting the words which excluded the criminal from participation in public prayers. Michael understood his dangerous position; he acknowledged his guilt, feigned to submit to the anathema, and implored pardon of his judge.

Whilst the emperor was devoting his attention to the restoration of Constantinople, Michael, Despot of Epirus, was devastating the country, taking cities, and even advancing boldly to the frontiers of the empire. Palæologus sent Alexis Strategopulus to oppose him. But the Cæsar after obtaining some unimportant advantage was defeated, and fell into the hands of his enemy. The Despot sent him as a present to his son-in-law, Manfred, King of Sicily, who claimed him for the purpose of strangling him, with his sister Anne, widow of the emperor Vataces.

The cruelty exercised upon the young Lascaris had roused in the souls of the Greeks a just indignation, but they gave no open expression to their discontent. The mountaineers of the environs of Nicæa, simple and rural men, were the only ones who raised the standard of revolt, and having met a child of nine years of age rendered blind by disease, they imagined him to be the young Lascaris, the prince whom they had sworn to defend with their lives. They conveyed him to the mountains, clothed him in royal garments, surrounded him with guards, paid him the honors due a sovereign, and promised to avenge him, to the great astonishment of the boy, who knew not what they meant. Hearing of this strange insurrection, Palæologus sent troops against the rebels. It was impossible to force their mountain defences; but the greater part were won over by presents, and after the flight of the pretended Lascaris to the Turks, the revolt died out.

On returning from an expedition against the Sultan of Iconium, Palæologus seriously considered the means of inducing Arsenius to remove the excommunication fulminated against him. He tried in every way to disarm the anger of the Patriarch. He begged of him any penance he chose to impose, promising to submit to it. He cast himself at the feet of the prelate, but the only answer vouchsafed to his entreaties was: "*Do what you can to efface the crime you have committed.*" The inflexible Arsenius refused to appoint any means of expiation, saying that great sins demanded a great atonement. "Must I then," said Palæologus, "abdicate the throne?"

Saying these words, he drew his sword and offered to resign it to the patriarch, who extended his hand to receive it. The emperor, however, who was not prepared to pay so dear for his absolution, returned his sword to the scabbard, and continued his supplications. Then Arsenius indignantly withdrew into an inner apartment, leaving the suppliant emperor outside the door.

After these humiliating attempts, Michael, despairing of overcoming the determination of the Patriarch, complained openly of his harshness. He assembled the bishops, and adroitly intimated to them that if they had no canon for the remission of sin, he might possibly find a more indulgent judge at Rome. The frightened prelates sent a deputation to Arsenius begging him to be more clement; but the deputies were coldly received and reproached for their condescension to a criminal prince. A synod, in consequence, deposed Arsenius, and a guard of soldiers conducted him to the island of Proconesia, where he was permitted to see no one (1266). Germain, Bishop of Adrianople, a man of letters, of agreeable address and good morals, was called to the See of Byzantium. But the mildness of the new Patriarch displeased the people and increased the partisans of Arsenius; besides, Germain of himself had no power to absolve the emperor. He abdicated the patriarchal throne the very year of his election (1267), and retired to a small dwelling on the sea shore, determined to pass the remainder of his days in the peace of private life. The monk Joseph, confessor of Palæologus, succeeded him. Loaded with honors by his sovereign,

Joseph withdrew the anathema, and restored the penitent to the communion of the faithful. The first condition imposed upon the usurper was to alleviate the sufferings of the victim of his ambition. He assigned a large revenue to the unfortunate Lascaris, that he might live in luxury in the castle of Dacybize; and after his reconciliation with the Church, he deceitfully professed affection for this prince. But the spirit of Arsenius lived in his numerous partisans among the monks and clergy, and he was ever considered an intruder.

The new imperial residence had already become fatal to the provinces of the East. Palæologus, separated from Asia, did not pay sufficient attention to those portions of his empire which lay beyond the Bosphorus. Avaricious governors oppressed them, and after having devastated them, left them a prey to the Turks. Still these provinces would have been lost to the Greeks, had not the emperor sent thither his brother John, a prince honored with the title of despot, of tried valor and skill in the military art. John in a short time drove away this rapacious horde, and restored the ancient form of government; his courage and activity restrained the ever-increasing audacity of the Turks, whose depredations seemed to justify the prediction of old Senator Tornice. The preservation of the East required the presence either of the despot or of the emperor; but the former was almost always engaged in some expedition against the barbarians on the western frontier, and Palæologus was detained at Constantinople by the seditions of the partisans of Arsenius, who now formed in the state a powerful party, political as well as religious.

Michael, the Despot of Epirus, had, at his death, divided the state between his two sons; to Nicephorus, the elder, he left the ancient Epirus; but as he relied on the valor of John, he bequeathed him that portion which he would be obliged to contest with the empire, that is, all Thessaly, from Mount Olympus to Parnassus. This intriguing prince assumed the title of Duke of Patras, and soon possessed himself of the territory which his father had left him to conquer. Palæologus equipped a numerous army, entrusting the command to the despot John. This intrepid general carried by assault nearly all the important places in Thessaly. Incapable of making a stand against the troops of the enemy and deserted by his own men, the Duke shut himself up in Neopatras, his capital, which was immediately besieged. But his destruction was inevitable in a position where his provisions must necessarily soon fail. Then he makes a determination, inspired by the desperate condition to which he is reduced. Favored by the darkness of night, he escapes from the city in disguise, and hastening to John de la Roche, Grand Duke of Thebes and Athens, he obtains from him five hundred Athenian cavaliers, and falling suddenly upon the army of the despot, puts it to flight. The conquered prince could not pardon himself for this reverse; he divested himself of the insignia of his dignity, and by this voluntary degradation became a simple citizen (1271).

About this period, Andronicus, the eldest son of the emperor, having attained his fifteenth year, married the daughter of Stephen V., King of Hungary. This marriage was blessed by the patriarch Joseph in the church of St. Sophia, and celebrated at Constantinople by festivities in which Palæologus displayed the most unbounded magnificence. Eager to secure the succession to his family, he decided the following year to share the honors of the purple with Andronicus, who was accordingly crowned and solemnly proclaimed emperor of the Romans. He bore this august title during a long and inglorious reign, nine years as his father's colleague and fifty years as his successor.

Michael was continually beset both by foreign and domestic enemies. His conquest of Constantinople and his residence in that capital seemed a bold defiance to all those Latins who had overthrown the Greek empire and shared the spoils under the Pontificate of Innocent III. The Venetians, particularly, were not disposed to accept without a struggle the loss of their numerous possessions. In order to profit by the rivalry existing between the Venetians and Genoese, the emperor stirred up between these two maritime powers a war which might prevent the Venetians from taking up arms against the Greeks. By strong representations on the subject of this alliance, and by the excommunication of the Genoese, Urban IV. notified Palæologus both of the danger which menaced him and of the means of averting it. The reunion of the Greek Church with the Church of Rome would please the West, and excite their interest in the perilous condition of the empire. Moreover, the brother of Louis IX., Charles of Anjou, who at that time became King of Sicily, acquired in 1267, by a treaty with the deposed emperor Baldwin II., a claim upon the throne of Byzantium for his daughter Beatrix, the claim reverting to himself. The Pope. who was suzerain of the King of Sicily, could, by the influence he exercised over his vassal, either arm or restrain the Christian prince. It was therefore of the utmost importance to the emperor to conciliate his good will.

Michael assembled the clergy in his palace, and notwithstanding the opposition he met with, he proposed a reunion with Gregory X. He did not conceal from them that the very existence of the empire was at stake, and that he looked to this reunion as a means of salvation. Irritated by the resistance of the bishops, he promulgated an edict in which he declared that in taking Constantinople by force of arms he had become the proprietor of all the houses in the city; that he would permit all who would obey him to occupy them free of rent, but that payment would be exacted of his opponents. Some gave in their adhesion because they had not the means of making payment; others went into voluntary exile; a part were punished by the imperial authority, and endured the most ignominious outrages; the people, in general, were unshaken in their opposition. Joseph, the usurping patriarch, published a pastoral letter in which he swore that he would never consent to reunion; Arsenius, the deposed patriarch, fulminated from his place of exile a new excommunication against the emperor, delivered him over to Satan, and died without changing his sentiments.

The emperor remained immovable in his determination; an embassy composed of ministers and prelates upon whom he could rely, embarked for Italy (1274), bearing offerings to St. Peter's church, precious ornaments, perfumes and jewels. The two galleys conveying the ambassadors and their numerous suite were overtaken by a storm; one struck upon the rocks, and the rich presents sent by the emperor to Gregory X., were engulfed in the sea. The Pope received the envoys of Michael Palæologus in the General Council of Lyons at the head of five hundred bishops, and shedding tears of joy, gave them the kiss of peace. The Greek prelates, headed by Germain, the last Patriarch of Constantinople, sang the Creed and thrice repeated that the *Holy Ghost proceeded from the Father and the Son.* Three conditions were proposed and accepted: "The Pope shall be named in public prayer; appeals to the Court of Rome shall be allowed, and the primacy of the Pope acknowledged." At the conclusion of the Council, the ambassadors returned, satisfied with the honors which had been bestowed upon them. According to the custom of the Latin Church, the Pope had decorated the prelates with the ring and mitre. They arrived at Constantinople in the autumn of the same year.

But no sooner had the name of the Pope been mentioned at mass under the title of Universal Bishop, than the patriarch Joseph, the prelates and monks, and the body of the people, openly declared against union. Joseph resigned his See, and retired into a monastery. He was replaced by Veccus, an ecclesiastic of known moderation, in whom Palæologus had great confidence (1275). But the efforts of the monarch met with little success, only a few courtiers and priests yielding to his wishes.

Some years later, Pope Nicholas III., suspecting the sincerity of the Greeks, sent legates to Constantinople with instructions to require a profession of faith from all the ecclesiastics of the empire. The emperor was much embarrassed: he feared, should the Holy Father become displeased, that he might yield to the urgent entreaties of Charles of Anjou, and permit him to attack Constantinople, and yet he failed to obtain from the clergy the profession of faith. Palæologus had recourse to stratagem and endeavored to deceive the Pope's legates. He solemnly promised the Greek prelates that he would permit no change in their customs nor the least addition to the Creed of their fathers, advised them to deal prudently with the legates, and to settle the difficulty by fair words. By this means he obtained from them a formula in which ambiguous phrases interspersed with sentences from Scripture apparently contained a declaration of Catholic faith. In a long discourse, Palæologus explained to the ennoys all he had done and suffered in order to consummate the union of the Greek with the Latin Church. That they might have no doubt as to the punishment inflicted by his orders upon the sectaries, whatever their rank might be, he directed Isaac, Bishop of Ephesus, to imprison the Latin prelates, which being done, the legates were conducted to the dungeons, where they found four princes of the imperial family—Andronicus Palæologus, Raoul Manuel, his brother Isaac, and John Palæologus, nephew of Andronicus—in chains in a narrow prison, in consequence of their resistance to reunion. The emperor even sent to the Pope two of the most obstinate schismatics, to be punished as he should think fit. Nicholas III. sent them back to the emperor, recommending him to be clement; at the same time he retained his suspicions of Michael's sincerity.

At Constantinople Michael was detested on account of his cruelty—he had during a journey into Natolia, put out the eyes of two princes, his prisoners: his favorite generals, his sister Eulogia, his nieces and other members of his family deserted his cause, which they regarded as sacrilegious; at Rome he was doubted. At last Pope Martin IV., successor of Nicholas III. (1281), publicly excommunicated Michael Palæologus and his adherents as barbarians, who had shown no mercy to the unfortunate. The only revenge taken by the emperor, was to forbid on a festival day, the mention of the Pope's name at mass.

A league to dethrone Palæologus was formed between Philip, the Latin emperor, heir of Baldwin II., the Venetians, and Charles of Anjou, king of the two Sicilies, whose sword had hitherto remained in its scabbard at the bidding of Gregory X. The brother of Sain t Louis gave the command of his troops to Soliman Rossi, a nobleman of Provence. He obtained possession of Albania and attacked the fortress of Belgrade. Palæologus hastened to its relief. Rossi was conquered and made prisoner. Taking advantage of the consternation caused by this first defeat, the Greeks brought all their forces into open field, and in a general battle. victory crowned their efforts. But the emperor, aware that he could not rely on his troops, trusted for success to the conspiracy headed by John de Procida, which later was to snatch Sicily from the grasp of his most powerful adversary.

As soon as he was relieved from the anxiety caused him by Charles of Anjou, Palæologus turned his attention to those neighboring princes who had provoked his anger; among them was the Prince de Sayes, who continued to assume the title of Emperor of Trebizond. His next expedition was against the Prince of Thessaly, who had broken the truce then existing between them. Having arrived at a small village in Thrace, he died suddenly at the age of fifty-eight (1282), but little regretted by his subjects. A few days before his death he learned with joy the revolt of Sicily against Charles of Anjou and the victory of Peter of Aragon, an event which secured the independence of Sicily and the preservation of the throne of the Palæologi. His son Andronicus, whom he had named as his successor, was proclaimed Emperor of the East.

Andronicus II., the Elder, definitively broke the temporary union of the two churches. He recalled at once the Greek prelates from exile, deposed Veccus, and restored Joseph, now an infirm old man, to the partriarchate of Constantinople. The temples were purified, penitents reconciled, and the new emperor not only refused his father the funeral ceremonies due from a son, but even denied him Christian burial. Upon the death of Joseph, shortly after his return, the patriarchal dignity was conferred on Gregory, who, being soon compelled to abdicate, was succeeded by the monk Athanasius.

The Mussulmans in the mean time had been making rapid progress, and seemed to threaten with destruction the very throne of Andronicus. The emperor was not powerful enough to cope with them unaided, and he was forced to hire the mercenary troops of Roger de Flor. These were composed of Sicilians, Catalonians, and Aragonese, who had fought on sea and land for the houses of Aragon or Anjou, and who, upon the restoration of peace, were left unemployed. For twenty years they had been engaged in warfare; their country was the field of battle or the ship of war. When on the point of engaging in contest, they struck the ground with their swords, exclaiming: "Sword, awake!" Roger set sail from Messina, and steered for Constantinople with a fleet of four large vessels and eighteen galleys, bearing eight thousand of his intrepid warriors. The emperor lodged the valiant Roger in a palace, bestowed upon him the title of grand-duke or admiral of Roumania, and gave him his niece in marriage. After a short repose they passed into Asia, where the success of their first campaign far surpassed the hopes of Andronicus, and two brilliant victories over the Turks, one near Cyzicus, the other near Mount Taurus, obtained for their chief the surname of Liberator of the East. The arrival of another adventurer, Berenger of Eutenca (1306), and the good understanding existing between Roger and himself, would undoubtedly have saved the empire many calamities if the Greeks had been able to act without perfidy.

Victorious over the Turks, Roger became an object of dread to the pusillanimous allies; he demanded of the emperor his recompense, who, not having at command the treasures with which the Comneni had purchased the aid of the Prussans and Normans, paid the troops in counterfeit coin. On his refusal to disband his army, he was invited to a banquet at the royal palace of Adrianople, and killed by the order of Michael, who had received from his father, Andronicus, the honors of the purple. At the news of this crime, the adventurers, abandoning themselves to transports of fury, swore the destruction of the Greeks and massacred the inhabitants of Gallipoli. Berenger of Eutenca ravaged the coasts of the Propontis and attempted to burn the vessels of his perfidious allies in the harbor of Constantinople. Unfortunately he was defeated and made prisoner by the Genoese. The Catalans elected for their chief Raccafort, son-in-law of Roger, and their forces, bearing the title of *Army of the Franks, Rulers of Thrace and Macedonia*, crushed the imperial troops sent to opose them, and soon became masters of all Thrace. For five years (1307–1312), they were a terror to Constantinople, but were, at last, forced by the dissensions among their chiefs and want of provisions, to remove from the environs of the capital. Andronicus esteemed himself fortunate in being able to turn the course of this dreaded soldiery towards the Duchy of Athens, which was soon subdued. The victorious Catalans divided Bœotia and Attica among themselves, and for fourteen years were the scourge of Greece. They then disappear from history, but the remembrance of their devastations remained long engraved upon the minds of the Greeks and passed into the proverb: *May the vengeance of the Catalans overtake you!*

Freed from these anxieties, Andronicus the Elder, whose long reign is remarkable only for the contentions of the Greek Church, the invasion of the Catalans, and the increase of the Ottoman power, was called upon to defend his crown against the impatience of his grandson, Andronicus the Younger. The premature death of Michael, his father (1320), assured him of obtaining ere long the imperial dignity; but fearing lest his dissipation and extravagance might induce his grandfather to transfer the crown to another of his grandsons, he raised the standard of revolt. John Cantacuzenus was the counsellor and general of the young debauchee, whose triumph he secured after a contest of five years (1328). Deprived of all power, the deposed monarch changed the purple for the monk's habit, and died in a cloister.

CHAPTER II.

CIVIL DISCORD—PROGRESS OF THE OTTOMANS.

Weakness of the Empire of the East—Commencement of the power of the Ottoman Turks—Reign of Othman—Conquest of Prusa—Orkhan—His progress—Discord of the Greeks—Orkhan marries the daughter of Cantacuzenus—The latter enters Constantinople—His moderation—John Palæologus marries the Princess Helena—Orkhan visits his father-in-law at Scutari—Civil war between the two Emperors—Establishment of the Ottomans in Europe—Palæologus sole Emperor—Conquest of Soliman—His death—Grief and death of Orkhan—Amurat I.—Success of the Ottomans—Occupations of Amurat during peace—Organization of the Janizaries—Defeat of the King of Hungary—John Palæologus in the West—Conspiracy of Andronicus and Saoudji discovered and punished—Amurat takes Thessalonica—Andronicus is proclaimed emperor—He returns to his allegiance—Battle of Cassora—Death of Amurat I.—Bajazet I. his successor—Humiliation of the Emperor—His death.

AFTER having escaped falling into the power of Chosroes and other enemies equally dreaded, the city of Constantine had recovered under some of her emperors an apparent strength which, however, covered a real weakness. Unskilled in arms, the people seemed to forget the implacable enemies who threatened her, and who awaited only a favorable opportunity to overthrow an empire already undermined by revolutions and corruption of morals. Strange to say, the degenerate Cæsars, absorbed in continual dissensions and surrounded by luxuries, looked with indifference upon the terrible drama which was being enacted, and they did not perceive that it necessarily involved the loss of their crown. If at times they awoke from their lethargy and listened to the distant mutterings of the storm, they consoled themselves by thinking it was remote, and then relapsed into their fatal lethargy. Therefore, after the abdication of Cantacuzenus, historical interest attaches exclusively to the Ottomans, who, docile to the voice of their skillful and valiant chiefs, were soon to deal the last blow to the decrepit empire of Constantinople. Let us then consider this new people, destined by Providence to replace in Europe and Asia the degenerate race of Greeks.

The domination of the Seljuk dynasty in Asia Minor no longer existed; upon the death of the brave Aladin, their last Sultan, their empire, already subjugated by the Moguls, was divided by the emirs into ten independent states. The most powerful of the emirs was Caraman, who left the name Caramania to the portion of the southern coast of Asia Minor which had fallen to his share, and Othman, the son of Orthogrul, who imposed his name upon the Turkish horde whom he commanded. Gifted with all the qualifications of a good soldier, Othman, taking advantage of circumstances, led his followers into the plains of Bithynia and Paphlagonia. According to the Turkish account, the lofty destiny of his posterity was made known to him in a dream. One night as he lay asleep in the house of the Cheik Edebali, he had the following vision: He beheld himself and his host extended side by side, both in a deep sleep. From the breast of the cheik he saw the moon, the star of Mahomet, arise and increase visibly until it became full, when it descended and entered his breast. From his body sprang a tree with firm and solid roots, with strong branches of extraordinary beauty, which lengthened as though to cover all lands and seas. The shadow of this tree fell upon three parts of the earth as far as the horizon. Under its shelter arose high mountains, the Caucasus, Atlas, Taurus and Hemus, which resembled the four columns of the eternal tent. From the roots of the tree flowed the Tigris, Euphrates, Nile, and Danube, covered with vessels as the sea. The fields were rich with harvests, the mountains covered by thick forests whence gushed out numerous springs watering the flowery meadows and the arbors of roses of this Eden. In the valleys his eye dwelt upon cities ornamented with domes, cupolas, pyramids, obelisks, magnificent columns and lofty towers, upon the summit of which glistened the Crescent; from galleries arose the call to prayer mingling with the chant of an infinite multitude of nightingales and the chattering of parrots, variegated with a thousand different colors. The various inhabitants of the air sang and warbled in the interwoven branches and amid the countless leaves, all cut in the form of a sabre. Next a strong wind blew which turned the points of these leaves towards the different cities of the world, and principally towards the city of Constantine, which, situated at the junction of two seas and two continents, resembled a diamond encased between two sapphires and two emeralds, and seemed thus to form the most brilliant stone of the ring of a vast domination embracing the whole world. Othman was about to place the ring upon his finger when he awoke. This tree was the emblem of the son of Orthogrul, the true founder of the race and domination of the *Osmanlis* or Ottomans.

The new conqueror crossed the Hellespont, and his presence spread terror throughout the Chersonesus, whence the inhabitants fled and left the land uncultivated for ten months. Having taken Iconium from the Mogols, Othman attacked the brave knights of St. John of Jerusalem, in the island of Rhodes where they had just established themselves, but he was repulsed by a Frenchman, Foulquis de Villaret, Grand-master of the order (1315). He soon recovered from this blow, deriving his advantage from the internal dissensions of the Greek empire, and during the twenty-seven years of his reign, he was successful in all his incursions and subdued a large portion of the states of the Seljukian Turks. The conquest of Prusa, one of the most important cities of Asia Minor, by his son Orkhan, was the crowning glory of his arms. Proud of having won a capital and a tomb worthy of him, Othman died the same year (1326), loaded with honor and venerated by the Ottomans, who attributed to him all the great qualities which usually fall to the lot of founders of an empire. As he was about to breathe his last, he gave his parting instructions to Orkhan, his eldest son, who was to succeed him, recommending him to avoid tyranny in governing, to regard justice as the firmest foundation of his throne, to be the protector of his people, and to rule with equity and mildness. Four months before his death, he had consigned to the grave his father-in-law, the Cheik Edebali, and a month later his cherished wife, Malchatum.

The Ottoman empire may properly date from the fall of Prusa. Ascending the throne between the coffin of a father and the cradle of a son, crowned with the laurels of a recent victory, Orkhan transformed this city into a Mohammedan capital. He built a mosque, a hospital and a college, over which presided learned professors, who attracted to it Persian and Arabian students from the schools of the East. His first act was to offer to divide the wealth left by his father with his brother Aladin, who, however, refused to accept even the half of the horses, cattle and sheep, requesting only for his residence a village situated in the plain of Prusa, on the western shore of the Nilufer. "At least," said Orkhan, "since you refuse to possess either horses, cattle or sheep, be a shepherd of my people, I mean a vizir." Aladin, yielding to the wishes of his sovereign, became the first vizir of the empire, and shared with the prince the cares of the government. Inexperienced in military life, Aladin devoted himself entirely to the civil administration, and by wise institutions gave stability to the empire, whilst his brother extended it by new conquests. Orkhan directed a particular dress for the soldiery to distinguish them from the citizens, ordering that they should have the exclusive right to wear a white turban. He coined money stamped with his own name, and removed from circulation the pieces bearing the impress of the Seljukians of Iconium.

The troops of Othman had been composed of bodies of Turcoman cavalry, who served without pay and fought without discipline. He had given the precedent of recruiting his army from captives and volunteers. His son determined to perfect this system and to form a soldiery who, abjuring their country, family and religion, should, in future, regard the will of their chief and a passive obedience as their country, family, and religion. In pursuance of this idea, he ordered Christian children made prisoners in infancy or before they had come to the use of reason, to be brought up in Islamism; and of these unfortunate orphans who knew no other profession than arms he formed a formidable body, to which the Ottomans, in a great measure, owed their success. Their numbers amounted at first to twenty-five thousand men, and by the care and intelligence of Orkhan they were provided with machines constructed by skillful workmen for besieging and assaulting cities.

Orkhan, pursuing his victorious career in Asia Minor, obtained possession of Nicomedia in 1328, of Nicæa five years later, and subjugated the whole of Bithynia as far as the shores of the Bosphorus and the Hellespont. At this period the throne of Constantinople was occupied by Andronicus III., who at last enjoyed the object of his ambition. This prince was skilled in the art of war, and endowed with extreme activity. His favorite, Cantacuzenus, encouraged him by his counsels, and urged him to great exertion. An army sent by the son of Othman against the Greeks was defeated at Trajanopolis (1330), and later Andronicus and Cantacuzenus drove back thirty-six vessels which were advancing against Constantinople. But the emperor's passion for theological discussions deprived him of aid from the West. A few monks, maintaining with bitterness some silly reveries, were condemned by a council held at St. Sophia. Andronicus III. could not resist taking part in the quarrel, and died from excessive fatigue after a violent discussion, leaving the crown to a son nine years old, John 1st Palæologus, of whom Cantacuzenus was appointed guardian.

The favorite, who had never ceased to aid his master by his counsel and labors, who had refused the crown which the emperor during an illness had urged him to accept after the death of Andronicus, gave free scope to his ambitious desires. He at first expressed his unwillingness to exercise the charge of regent, under pretense that the office was coveted by John of Apri, and he yielded at last only to the reiterated request of the empress mother, after exacting from her an oath that she would not be influenced against him by the calumnies of his enemies. He studiously concealed his aspirations to the throne. Having subdued the Latins of Peloponnesus, and imposed a tribute upon them, the regent returned to Constantinople to crush the powerful faction of his adversaries, at the head of which were the Patriarch and grand chamberlain, Apocauque. Being called from the city a second time to superintend the preparation of an expedition to be sent against the Latins of the south and the Prince of Persia, who was devastating Macedonia, Cantacuzenus was informed that the empress, yielding to the solicitations of Apocauque, had joined the ranks of his enemies, that his mother and his family were detained as prisoners in their own house under strict guard, and that he himself had been declared a public enemy. He offered to deliver himself to the empress, and to trust the result of an investigation to her decision, but the soldiers urged him to make war; the chiefs were eager to support him, and persuaded him to assume the title of emperor. He was crowned at Didymoticus, and the greater part of Thrace and Macedonia declared in his favor.

The new Cæsar was obliged to turn his attention to organizing his army, and selecting chiefs who would be devoted to his interests. When, however, the city of Adrianople abandoned his cause, he offered peace to his enemies. But his envoys were coldly received at Constantinople, and the empress, although inclined to effect a reconcilation, was forced by Apocauque to declare war. A second time Cantacuzenus sent monks from Athos to solicit peace, and again the Patriarch caused his proposition to be rejected. At the same time the court displayed the greatest energy. Apocauque crowned the young emperor, who in return bestowed upon him the title of Grand Duke. Some of the relatives of Cantacuzenus were put to death, and his mother, cast into prison, died from the effects of ill-treatment. The usurper, determining to prosecute the war with the utmost vigor, sought to secure his revenge by soliciting foreign aid, and he made an alliance with the Prince of Servia and the Khan of Lydia, Oumour-Beg, whom the knights of Rhodes, the real defenders of the Christian name, recalled by menacing Smyrna, his capital (1343).

Another Turkish ally more powerful than Oumour-Beg solicited the hand of the daughter of Cantacuzenus. This was Orkhan, whose assistance was at that time sought by the empress mother, Anne of Savoy; he pledged himself to fulfil towards the regent all the duties incumbent upon a subject and a son, if he would accept him for his son-in-law. The ambitious Cantacuzenus gave his daughter Theodora in marriage to the prince of the Ottomans. Orkhan sent thirty vessels bearing the highest nobles of his court, accompanied by a large body of cavalry, to form an escort for his imperial bride. The father of Theodora surrounded by the grand dignitaries and his family, met them before the camp of Selymbria. In front of the city was erected a magnificent pavilion, under which the empress Irene passed the night with her three daughters. Early in the morning the young bride, according to an ancient custom of the Byzantine court, ascended a platform hung with the richest tapestry. The troops were under arms, the emperor at their head on a charger superbly caparisoned, and attended by the imperial guard. At a given signal the heavy silk curtains embroidered in gold thread which encircled the throne were withdrawn, and the bride appeared in the midst of numerous attendants bearing nuptial torches. Immediately the air resounded with the music of trumpets and other instruments, and various choirs united in song to celebrate the virtues of the daughter of Cæsar. The festivities continued for several days, during which the Greeks and Turks mingled together as brethren (1346).

About the same time Cantacuzenus was delivered from his most bitter enemy. Apocauque had cast into prison all against whom he entertained the slightest suspicion. Some of the prisoners succeeded in loosening their chains, and one day when he went to visit them, they fell upon him, put him to death, and freed their companions in misfortune.

Upon the discovery of several conspiracies formed against his life, Cantacuzenus considered that it was necessary to strike a decisive blow and consummate his usurpation by taking possession of the capital. Communicating with his numerous partisans within the city, a day was appointed upon which they were to throw open the Golden Gate to give him entrance. He presented himself at the head of his army, and he was admitted without opposition. He proposed terms to the empress, who at first refused to consider any proposition, but yielding at last to the entreaties of her son, fifteen years of age, she accepted the conditions of the conqueror. It was agreed by both parties that there should be a general amnesty, that the two emperors should reign jointly, the younger to be guided for ten years by the advice of the elder. So great was the moderation of Cantacuzenus that it was a subject of astonishment to all. He boasts of it himself, saying: "Who could believe that after having suffered so much from his enemies, he did not profit by his victory to destroy them; that when he might have annihilated the vanquished, he treated with them as his equals? Such a course of conduct indicates something superior to human nature."

Cantacuzenus continued to exhibit himself as the mildest of usurpers. But notwithstanding his respectful deportment, his presence always intimidated the empress; he strove by every means in his power to reassure her, even offering in marriage his daughter Helen to the young emperor. The proposal was accepted, and from that time the reconciliation appeared sincere.

In the meantime Cantacuzenus was much disturbed by the successes of the Prince of Servia, who had ravaged Macedonia, and he found it necessary to convene the States in order to obtain supplies. He was also troubled by the conduct of his eldest son Matthias, who, listening to evil counsel, possessed himself of Didymoticus and Adrianople, with the intention of establishing an independent principality. He was persuaded by his mother to abandon his odious design, but the joy of the father at this act of obedience was clouded by the death of his youngest son, who was carried off by the plague in 1348.

The same year Orkhan, accompanied by his family and the officers of his court, visited his father-in-law at Scutari, and for some days the two princes enjoyed together with apparent cordiality the pleasures of the chase and the festivities of the court. Cantacuzenus and Orkhan were seated at one table, the four sons of the Ottoman chief occupied another at a short distance, and surrounding them the Turks and Greeks were placed upon carpets extended upon the ground. Orkhan remained in the camp near the fleet, whilst Cantacuzenus went to Constantinople with his daughter, Theodora, who passed three days with her mother and sisters. The son-in-law of the emperor returned to Bithynia with his family, loaded with presents. But the friendship of Orkhan was subordinate to his political or religious interests, and in the war against the Genoese he did not hesitate to join the enemies of his father-in-law.

Later, with the aid of Pasha Soliman, eldest son of Orkhan, Cautacuzenus retook from the despot of Servia, Thessalonica, Burhœa and the greater part of Macedonia. The young emperor wished to contract an alliance with the conquered prince, with the hope of becoming sole master of the throne; but the usurper opposed his design and restrained his ambition for some time through the influence of the widow of Andronicus III. But when the princes of Servia and Bulgaria and the Republic of Venice had espoused the cause of John Palæologus, he resolved to apply to the Ottomans, who were, at last, about to secure a firm foothold in Europe.

Having returned to Asia, Soliman was seated one evening on the eastern shore of the Propontis; the moonlight cast upon the sea the shadow of the ruins of the ancient Eyzieus, a colony of Milesians famous in Grecian and Roman history, which after many vicissitudes, in a long struggle with the great powers of the universe, had become a second time the capital of the province of the Hellespont. With his eyes fixed upon the clear waters in which were mirrored the marble porticos, the avenues of columns, the stately ruins of the temples of Cybele, of Proserpine and Jupiter, over which flitted the clouds of the sky, he meditated upon this departed grandeur, and he seemed to behold palaces and temples arising from the abyss, and fleets sailing proudly over the waters. Mingling with the murmur of the waves he heard mysterious voices, from the moon in the east he saw descending a silver streamer which floated over the abyss and united Europe and Asia. It was the same luminary which, having formerly arisen from the breast of Edebali had sunk into the breast of Othman. This dream had presaged to his grandfather the empire of the world; the remembrance aroused his courage, and from that moment he determined to unite Europe to Asia by the force of arms.

Having consulted the old men who had grown gray in the service of his family, and having long devised some means to traverse the straits secretly, he at last ventured to cross in a boat with a friend, and pushed on towards Tympa to reconnoitre the country, proceeding beyond Gallipoli. There he seized a Greek, whom he took with him to Mysia to employ him as a guide. Informed by the Greek, who proved a traitor to his countrymen, of the defenseless condition of the castle, he formed the project of surprising it. The following night, embarking with fifty-nine determined soldiers, he succeeded in capturing the fort of Tzympe, and this the more easily because on account of the harvest the inhabitants were dispersed through the fields. In the course of a few days he had garrisoned the fort with three thousand men (1356).

Whilst the Ottomans were thus establishing themselves at Tzympe, Cantacuzenus had begged the assistance of Orkhan against John Palæologus; yielding to his solicitations he sent Soliman at the head of ten thousand Turkish cavaliers, who landed at the mouth of the Maritza. The impetuosity of the Mohammedan troops could not be restrained, and they committed great disorders; Soliman, having crushed the Bulgarians and the Servian auxiliaries of John Palæologus, returned to Asia loaded with booty. Then Cantacuzenus demanded of this prince the restitution of Tzympe in consideration of a thousand ducats. The emperor had despatched the gold, and Soliman had given orders to surrender the castle, when a frightful earthquake destroyed the walls and fortresses of the greater part of the cities of Thrace. The houses of Gallipoli were overthrown, and the breaches made in the walls offered an easy entrance to the soldiers, whose projects of pillage and conquest were thus favored by the earthquake (1357). At the same time other places, such as Konour, Boulair, Malgora, celebrated for its honey, Kypsale, a short distance from Gallipoli, and Rodosta, where the Thracian prince Rhesus had formerly reigned, admitted new Turkish colonies. Whilst complaining of the violation of the treaties, Cantacuzenus offered forty thousand ducats for the ransom of these places, particularly of Gallipoli, the key of the Hellespont, which he was averse to abandoning to the Turks. Orkhan promised to persuade his son to restore these cities, but he always evaded any definite settlement of the question. That very year the abdication of Cantacuzenus secured to the Ottomans their first conquest in Europe.

The affection of the people for John Palæologus exhibited itself on many occasions, and his efforts to make himself the emperor were crowned with success. In spite of his exertions to the contrary, his father-in-law had proclaimed his son Matthias emperor. Aided by a noble Genoese, to whom he had promised his sister in marriage, and furnished with two galleys mounted by twenty-five hundred men, he entered Constantinople. The arrival of the young emperor agitated the capital; men were uncertain what step to take, hesitating between their good feeling towards their prince and the fear of Cantacuzenus, who had under his orders disciplined troops of Catalonians. But weary of civil war, the usurper himself proposed peace. Three days later a treaty was signed between the two emperors, according to which they were to possess an equality of power; hardly was it signed when, to the astonishment of all, Cantacuzenus, renouncing the crown, divested himself upon the spot of the imperial ornaments, cut his hair and retired to the monastery of Mangana, where he assumed the name of Joseph. The empress Irene joyfully followed the example of her husband, received the veil with the name of Eugenia, and entered the convent of Martha.

Many reports in circulation attributed the retreat of this incomprehensible man to the violence of John Palæologus; but from the solitude of his cloister the new monk denied the charge and justified the conduct of his son-in-law. "Cantacuzenus," he said, "has abdicated the throne voluntarily, and he was not forced to take the step; had he wished to preserve it, no one could have taken it from him. Palæologus did not offend by the violation of his oath, and all must know that he did nothing to dissatisfy his father-in-law. Cantacuzenus acquired the throne unwillingly; he experienced many changes of fortune; he bore them with a spirit and courage which nothing could subdue. Having triumphed over his adversaries, he saw himself about to be plunged again into civil war; then he despaired of the Romans, from whom their ancient wisdom has departed, and he abdicated the empire."

From the depth of his retreat, where his unquiet spirit sought repose, Cantacuzenus exerted himself to maintain a good understanding between his son Matthias and Palæologus, who had promised to recognize this son as his colleague in the empire. Their hatred, restrained for a time, at last conducted them to the field of battle, in the plains of Philippa, a city of Thrace. Matthias was conquered, made prisoner, and sent under guard to the island of Lesbos. Palæologus offered him his liberty if he would lay aside the purple and descend to the second rank in the empire. Cantacuzenus emerged from his retreat to induce his son to accept the proposition of the emperor. He depicted to him in a powerful manner the dangers which surround the throne and the terrible responsibility of those who govern. Matthias consented, but most unwillingly, to make a formal renunciation of his claim.

The abdication of Cantacuzenus, the only man capable by his talents and wisdom of saving the empire, was a misfortune for the State. That skillful usurper understood how to hold in check or conquer his enemies. His last advice to his countrymen was such as induced them to avoid an imprudent war, and he bade them compare the number, discipline and enthusiasm of the Turks with the weakness of the Greeks. But the obstinate vanity of the young emperor despised this prudent advice, and the first year of the abdication Soliman crossed the straits, subjugated the cities which he attacked, possessed himself of the Chersonesus, and entered Thrace without opposition. In the midst of his brilliant achievements the hero lost his life by a fall from a horse during a military exercise. The tomb of the founder of the Ottoman power in Europe, erected on the shore of the Hellespont, seemed to invite the inhabitants of Asia to a pilgrimage of conquest. The aged Orkhan shortly afterwards died of grief caused by the loss of his grand vizier, his beloved son (1360). His reign of thirty-five years had been stained by no barbarity, by no murder. The political institutions of this just prince and valiant warrior have caused historians to name him the Numa of the Ottomans.

The Greeks had not time to congratulate themselves upon the death of their enemies; they found another still more terrible in the person of Amurat, eldest son of Orkhan and brother of Soliman. Ascending the throne at forty-one years of age, Amurat surpassed the most illustrious kings or commanders of armies by his promptness and indefatigable ardor in action. Repose was hateful to him, and when he had not enemies to contend with, he sought vent for his warlike disposition in the chase. Immediately upon his accession, he turned his attention to Asia, where he menaced and signalized his bravery by the conquest of Ancyra, a fortified city, a commercial centre which nature seemed to have favored in a particular manner. Having restored tranquillity in this quarter, he determined to follow up the conquests of his brother in Europe.

His experienced lieutenants became masters, almost without opposition, of Nebetos, Tscharli, Kechan, and Didymoticus. Adrianople, renowned for its advantageous situation at the junction of three rivers, fell the following year (1361). It afterwards ranked as the second capital of the Ottoman empire. Doriscus, Bershæa, Philippopolis, and a large number of their neighboring fortresses being reduced to obedience, gave to the Mussulmans a passage through Thrace to the north.

The uninterrupted successes of his enemies alarmed the Greek emperor: he asked for peace and obtained it. Amurat had, hitherto, following the example of his predecessors, dispensed himself from being present with the people at public prayer. A mufti, who is both priest and judge, had the boldness to punish him for this by refusing to admit his testimony in a civil suit brought before his tribunal. Astonished by such a procedure, Amurat demanded the cause: "My lord," said the mufti, "be not surprised at my conduct. As emperor, your word is sacred, and no one would dare to doubt it; but here it is of no value, a court of justice accepts not the testimony of a man who does not unite in public prayer with the body of Mussalmans." Amurat, intensely moved by the rebuke, acknowledged himself guilty, and in expiation of his fault constructed at Adrianople a sumptuous edifice opposite the imperial palace. The edifice preserves to this day the name of its founder.

About the same period Amurat gave a regular organization to the body of soldiery created by his father which was to be the terror of nations, and sometimes of the sultans themselves. He asked a celebrated dervish to bless them and select for them a banner and name (1362). Standing at the head of the ranks, the dervish extended the sleeve of his robe over the head of the soldier the nearest to him and said with solemnity: "Let them be called Janizaries (*yengi cheri*, or new soldiers). May their courage be always undoubted, their swords sharp, and their arms victorious! May their lances be ever ready to strike their enemies, and wherever they go, may they return to their homes from the dangers of war unharmed!"

The peace was not of long duration; the king of Hungary, Louis the Great, and the sovereigns of Servia, Bosnia and Wallachia, united to attack the conquerors from Asia, who were already menacing their frontiers. They advanced by forced marches as far as Maritya, about two days' march from Adrianople. The Ottoman victory was now complete, and the plain to this day is called *Sirf Vindrughi*, or defeat of the Servians (1363). This check of the warlike tribes of the Danube filled John Palæologus with the deepest anxiety. The emperor, a sad contrast to the majesty of Constantine the Great, left his capital and visited the west; he solicited from the Christian princes aid of men and money; he proclaimed his submission to the Church of Rome, abjured schism at Viterbo in the hands of Urban V. and promised to bring over all his subjects to the communion of the Latin Church. But he returned to the east unaccompanied by even one soldier. Deprived of all hope by the death of the aged Pontiff, he went to Venice, where he remained some time. As he was about to leave the city, he was arrested by some merchants who had lent him a considerable amount of money, and the august prisoner was restored to liberty only after his son Manuel had satisfied their demands by selling all he possessed.

Amurat marched from conquest to conquest; Ourosch, despot of Servia, having fallen in a battle against the nobles (1367), Boulks Lazarus was proclaimed his successor, but he was able to retain only southern Servia. Wonkassawitsch, who had occupied the northern part, was surprised by the Turks at night, and Amurat obtained possession of Acarnania and Servian Macedonia. He imposed a tribute upon the Greek emperor, and deprived him of Guistendil, a city founded by Trajan and of importance on account of its baths, its public buildings, and the gold and silver mines in its vicinity (1371). With equal activity he conquered the King of the Bulgarians, whose daughter he married, and Boulks Lazarus, who became his tributary.

Master of the Greeks, and already feared on the shores of the Danube, Amurat rested from his long continued toil. During an interval of six years, undisturbed by any warlike enterprise, he devoted himself unremittingly to the internal affairs of his kingdom, and bestowed particular attention upon the military organization. He divided the lands given to the Spahies into small fiefs (*timar*) and large fiefs (*siamet*), and to the proprietors of the former he gave the name of *timarli*. He instituted the *Voinaks*, troops composed of his Christian subjects, who in time of war performed the most humiliating functions. Amurat next summoned his tributary, John Palæologus, to accompany him in his expedition against Asia Minor. The emperor beheld the Christian King of Armenia despoiled of his states and condemned to exile; he saw the Seljoukian emir of Kermian bestow his daughter in marriage, with the finest portion of Phrygia for her dower, upon Bajazet, the eldest son of the formidable chief of the Ottomans. Hamid, prince of Pisidia, sold six cities for the privilege of preserving the small remainder of his dominions, and the emir of Caramania, defeated near Iconium, was compelled to pay tribute.

Whilst the emperor obtained pardon from Amurat by the basest submission, Andronicus, the eldest of his four sons, indignant because the direction of affairs had been taken from him and confided to Manuel, sought an opportunity for revenge. He found in Saoudji, the son of Amurat, who had temporary command of the Ottoman forces in Europe, a conformity of sentiments and character which soon united them in the closest friendship. Consumed by an ardent ambition, equally animated by a fierce hatred against their parents, these two princes conspired to seize the crown, and swore to be inviolably faithful to each other if they succeeded in their design. Upon receiving news of this infamous plot, Amurat summoned the unfortunate emperor before him, to render an account of the conduct of Andronicus. John Palæologus humbled himself, and in order to remove all suspicion of complicity with his son, he accepted the proposition made by his ally to march against the rebels, to make them prisoners and punish them for their revolt by the deprivation of sight. Amurat hastily crossed over into Europe, and overtook the revolted princes not far from Apricidion. He advanced on horseback during the night to their camp, and ordered them to surrender if they wished to obtain pardon. At the potent voice of their sovereign, the soldiers who had embraced the cause of Saoudji deserted in crowds, and implored the mercy of Amurat. The young prince, betrayed and abandoned, took refuge in Didymotica, with a small number of companions and the sons of those Greek nobles who remained faithful to him in his fallen fortunes. The father pursued him and beseiged the city. Famine forced the garrison to surrender, and Amurat exasperated by the obstinate resistance of Saoudji, ordered the executioners to put out his eyes first, and then to behead him. As to the Greek nobles, he commanded them to be tied together two and two and precipitated from the ramparts into the waters of the Maritza. From his camp he witnessed calmly this horrible execution.

Having satisfied his atrocious severity, Amurat sent an order to John Palæologus to punish his son in the same manner as he had punished Saoudji. The Greek obeyed. Andronicus, condemned to lose his sight by the injection of boiling vinegar into the eyes, escaped the full rigor of the punishment through the want of skill on the part of the executioner. Satisfied with the submission of the emperor in executing his orders, Amurat cared not to inquire if the accomplice of Saoudji had been totally deprived of sight. John Palæologus imprisoned the prince in the tower of Anemas with his wife and infant son, and designated Manuel as his successor, in place of his elder brother.

Manuel had fixed his residence at Thessalonica, of which city he was governor. Losing sight of the horrible catastrophe of Didymotica and the dangerous position of his father, who preserved his throne only by the most servile obedience, he conceived the project of taking from the Ottomans the important city of Pheræ. Amurat, informed of this treachery, despatched one of his best generals, Kaireddin Pasha, beyond the Bosphorus, with orders to take Thessalonica and to bring back Mauuel a prisoner. The ardor with which the Ottomans, far outnumbering the Greeks, pressed the siege, terrified the inhabitants. Always ready to revolt, they arose against Manuel and threatened to throw open the gates of the city to the enemy, if he did not obtain aid from Constantinople. The prince made known his unfortunate position to his father; the timid emperor returned for answer that he not only could afford him no aid, but that he dared not even receive him at his court for fear of incurring the anger of his dreaded ally. Deprived of all help, menaced on every side, Manuel escaped during the night upon a galley, and begged of the Genoese governor of Lesbos the asylum his father refused him in his palace. But there also the terror of the name of Amurat was so great that he was not permitted to land upon the island. He then formed the courageous resolution of going to Prusa, and throwing himself upon the mercy of the conqueror. This confidence of his enemy appeased the anger of

Amurat. He went out to meet him, mildly reproached him for his guilty conduct, generously granted the pardon he solicited, and sent him to his father, to whom he recommended kindness towards the heir of his throne. Thessalonica soon fell into the hands of the Turks.

The Greek empire declined daily; the Ottomans or their allies surrounded it on all sides; they already possessed the Chersonesus; a part of Thessaly belonged to them; only a breath was needed to overthrow the throne of Constantine. Although in so lamentable a condition, the Greeks did not refrain from civil discords. The rebel Andronicus, being delivered from his prison by the Genoese, was aided by these new allies to attack the emperor. He forced his father to capitulate and to admit him into Constantinople, after having solemnly sworn that he would renounce his odious projects. But violating his oath he soon proceeded to greater excesses than before. Supported by his partisans he proclaimed himself emperor, and imprisoned his father and brothers in the very house from which he had escaped. There they remained two years, when by the assistance of a friend they obtained their liberty and an asylum at Scutari. Andronicus, upon hearing this, pursued a course of conduct which filled the Greeks with astonishment; far from engaging in a sacrilegious war which might plunge the empire into the greatest disasters, he asked pardon of John Palæologus, declaring that he would no longer usurp the throne, and in proof of his sincerity he withdrew with all his family from Constantinople. The emperor, pacified by the submission of Andronicus, treated him kindly, and assigned him a small territory, whither he retired and lived tranquilly.

Whilst the empire was distracted by internal discord, Amurat, who had subdued Macedonia and Albania after a struggle of four years, saw himself menaced by a new storm on the side of Servia. The despot of Servia, Boulks Lazarus, had risen in revolt and united the Valakians, the Hungarians, the Dalmatians and the Triballians in a confederation against the Ottomans. This formidable league did not disquiet Amurat; he made his preparations for another expedition into Europe. But before taking the field, he sent to Lazarus a bag of millet as a sign of the countless troops he was directing against Servia; the despot scattered the grass to the fowl in the poultry-yard in presence of the ambassadors; then, addressing them, he said: "You see how quickly the fowl have devoured the millet; say to your master that his troops, however numerous they may be, shall, in like manner, be devoured by the Servians." He kept his word. An army of twenty thousand Ottomans was attacked by the combined forces of the allies, and totally routed. Amurat now took the command himself (1389); he deprived Sisman, King of Bulgaria, whose daughter he had married, of his states, and overtook the Servians at Cassova, on the frontiers of Bosnia and Servia.

Amurat passed a part of the night in deliberation with his most experienced generals and his two sons, Bajazet and Yacoub. He had confided the command of the right wing of the army to the former, and of the left to the latter. In the morning he gave the signal to advance. The shock of the opposing forces was terrible. The rage which animated both armies was so great that victory for a long time hung in the balance. The left wing of the Ottomans began to give way, when Bajazet hastened to their aid, opening a wide path for himself with his formidable club. In spite of their prodigies of valor, the Christians were defeated; a large number of their chiefs fell on the field of battle; Lazarus, overpowered by numbers, was made prisoner, with the greater part of the Servian nobles. After this victory, which annihilated the league and the independence of the Sclavonian tribes, Amurat went to visit the scene of carnage and recognize the dead. "How strange," he said to his Grand Vizir, Ali Pasha, "among all these dead I see only young men!" "To this we owe the victory," replied the vizir, "the rashness of youth listens only to the ardor which animates, and they die at our feet; men of mature age would not have ventured to oppose the invincible Ottomans." "It is the more surprising to me," continued Amurat, "that the event of the battle has been in our favor, and I am agreeably disappointed, for I dreamed last night that I was pierced through the body by the enemy." As he pronounced these words, a Triballian soldier sprang from amid the heap of dead bodies, plunged his dagger in his breast, and revenged the defeat of the Christians by the murder of the conqueror. The guards fell upon the soldier and killed him upon the spot. Amurat was borne to his tent, and died in pronouncing sentence of death against Lazarus and other Servian nobles. His remains were transported to Prusa, and deposited in the mosque constructed by his order.

This prince possessed some fine qualities. Notwithstanding the cruelty he exhibited in the execution of Saoudji and of the insurgents at Didymotica, his rare energy and superior intellectual powers cannot be denied. His love of justice and his simple tastes endeared him to his subjects.

The reign of Bajazet, the eldest son and successor of Amurat, was ushered in by a fratricide. In presence of the corpse of his father, he ordered the execution of the unfortunate Yacoub, who, having by his valor conciliated the affection of the army, had become an object of suspicion to him. Bajazet, surnamed *Ilderim* (lightning) by the Turks on account of the rapidity of his devastating incursions, perhaps surpassed Amurat himself, and certainly inspired more terror in the Christian world. He continued the war which his father had undertaken against Servia, compelled Stephen, the son of Lazarus, to swear fealty to him, and concluded a treaty with this prince by which the latter pledged himself to furnish a contingent in all the wars of the Ottomans, to give him his sister in marriage, and to pay an annual tribute. He next turned his attention to the humiliation of the Greeks. Having determined to obtain possession of Philadelphia, the only city remaining to them in Asia, he demanded aid from his new allies, the prince of Servia and the emperor of Constantinople. The governor of the place refusing to surrender to a barbarian and to accept a Turkish judge, John Palæologus and

Manuel were foremost in the attack upon their own city, and helped to deliver it up to Bajazet.

After subduing the emirs of Aidin, Saroukan, Kermian, and Casamania, and organizing the government of the conquered provinces, the sovereign of the Ottomans recrossed the Bosphorus in order to direct his forces against the princes of Europe. His first care was to fortify the city of Gallipoli and improve the harbor, after which he turned his steps towards the Archipelago. That the Greek emperor might be the witness of his new triumphs, he summoned him the first among his vassals to furnish his contingent. Manuel hastened as an humble vassal to the Ottoman court, at the head of a hundred men. Bajazet forbade the exportation of grain from Asia to the islands of Lesbos, Rhodes and Chios. A fleet of sixty large vessels sent against Chios reduced to ashes its cities and villages, devastated the other islands of the Archipelago, Euboea and a part of Attica.

John Palæologus, alarmed by the insolent manner in which Bajazet exercised his tyranny, meditated when too late upon the means of fortifying his capital. As he was destitute of materials, three of the most beautiful churches of Constantinople were demolished by his orders; the church founded by Leo the Philosopher, in honor of *All the Saints*, that of the *Forty Martyrs*, a monument of the piety of the emperor Marcian, and that of *Saint Moccius*, erected under Constantine the Great. It was with the enormous blocks of marble taken from these temples that he raised near the Golden Gate two lofty towers, afterwards dismantled by his own order, where in case of necessity he hoped to find a secure asylum. Informed of these preparations, Bajazet wrote to the emperor and expressed his will in the following terms: "You will without delay raze the newly-erected fortifications, or your son Manuel, having had his eyes put out, will return to you blind." John Palæologus, terrified by the danger which menaced the heir of his throne, obeyed the order; but the grief he felt at so cruel a humiliation, united to the sufferings of a violent attack of gout, caused his death shortly afterwards (1391). He was sixty-one years of age, weak, indolent and effeminate; he had not the energy for those great crimes which make men tyrants, nor for the great virtues which make good princes.

CHAPTER III.

BAJAZET AND TAMERLANE.

Manuel ascends the throne of Constantinople—Bajazet crosses into Europe—He ravages the empire, and menaces the capital—Crusade of Nicopolis—Defeat of the Christian army—Irruption of the Ottomans into Greece—Manuel divides the empire with his nephew—Expedition of Marshal Boucicaut—Manuel seeks aid from the kings of the West—His entry into Paris—He goes to England—His return to France—Inactivity of Bajazet—The approach of Tamerlane saves Constantinople—Expeditions of Tamerlane—Embassy from Tamerlane to Bajazet—The Sultan summons Manuel to surrender his capital—Siege and capture of Sebaste by the Moguls—Bajazet returns to Asia—Sack of Aleppo and Damascus—Destruction of Bagdad—Battle of Angora—Defeat and captivity of Bajazet—Efforts of his son ahomet to liberate him—Death of Bajazet—Return of Tamerlane to Samarcand—He dies on his march to China.

THE ruin of the empire was accelerated under Manuel, an enlightened statesman but an inefficient soldier, who succeeded John Palæologus at a moment when a hero was needed to uphold the tottering throne of the Cæsars. At the death of his father, Manuel was with Bajazet at Prusa, and not daring openly to claim his inheritance, he left the city secretly and returned to Constantinople. He was there acknowledged as emperor, and he celebrated the obsequies of his predecessor with the usual magnificence. Upon learning the escape of the Greek prince, the anger of Bajazet knew no bounds, and its first fury was vented upon the guards to whom he had been confided. But afterwards preferring to spare the life of the fugitive, that he might exact from him the most humiliating obedience, he dispatched one of his officers to bear him the following message: "In future a Mussulman cadi shall reside at Constantinople; for it is not proper that the true believers, when called to that city by business affairs, should be deprived of their own judges. Such is my will; if you refuse to obey me, remain within the precincts of your capital; all beyond it is mine."

The imperious Mussulman, considering the ambiguous answer of Manuel as equivalent to a refusal, passed from Bithynia into Thrace, devastated all the villages from Panidos to the very walls of Constantinople, and transported thence all the inhabitants into Asia. He next took Thessalonica and the places in its vicinity. From that moment in reality commenced the first siege or rather the first blockade of the capital of the Greek empire—a blockade which was to last five years. He left before its walls a body of troops, with directions to allow the Greeks no repose, but to harass them day and night. The rest of the army he divided into two corps, one of which entered Peloponnesus for the purpose of devasating Achaia and Lacedemon, and the other spread ruin throughout Roumania.

Peloponnesus was at that time governed by Theodore Palæologus, brother of the new emperor. This prince was distinguished by all the qualities which win for sovereigns the affection of their subjects. After restoring peace to his states, he devoted himself to the task of repairing the evils of war. Fame soon proclaimed his virtues and the mildness of his sway. Foreigners left their own country to go and settle in Peloponnesus, which had assumed a new aspect. Cities which had been abandoned were now populous and flourishing; desert fields were cultivated and yielded abundant harvests; forests which had served as retreats for brigands were cut down, and the land devoted to agriculture. In a word, nearly ten thousand Illyrians, driven from their own country by fear of the Turks, had found a home in Peloponnesus with their wives, children and flocks, and had become the faithful subjects of Theodore. With their aid he dispossessed the Turks of several important places, finally expelled them from his states, and gained a signal victory over a hostile prince of Achaia. To complete his happiness, Theodore obtained the hand of a daughter of the Duke of Athens, receiving with her as her dower the city of Corinth, one of the keys of the Peloponnesus. But these tranquil days were not of long duration; they did not escape the ascendency which the Turks regained in this country and in all the provinces of the empire.

Very soon there were neither reapers at Constantinople to mow the grain nor millers to grind the little they could purchase. To crush the city the tyrant did not overthrow the walls, nor batter them with powerful machines; but his soldiers dispersed in the environs exercised a constant vigilance, and guarded every outlet that nothing might be introduced or sent out of the capital, so that the want of grain, wine and oil was daily more seriously felt. Wood also was needed to cook the food, and they were obliged, in order to obtain it, to tear down their houses. Incapable of resisting the Ottoman power, Manuel wrote to the Pope, the Emperor of Germany, and the Kings of France and Hungary; he informed them of the power, ambition and successes of Bajazet, of the extremity to which Constantinople was reduced, and of the peril which threatened Europe should the progress of this terrible conqueror remain unchecked. He warned them that should they permit the wreck of the Greek empire to fall under the blows of the Mussulmans, the barbarians, having once broken down the barrier which obstructed their advance, would pour into the West and mark their path by blood and carnage.

In the meantime, Sisman, the Prince of Bulgaria, who had been deprived of his states, a part before, and a part after the battle of Cassova, despairing of prolonging the defence of Nicopolis, surrendered himself with his son in the camp of Ali Pasha, whither they went with a shroud cast around their neck to implore their lives. Sisman was sent as a prisoner to Philippopolis, and afterwards put to death. His son escaped punishment by embracing Islamism, and received in recompense of his apostasy the government of Amisus, a city of Asia recently subjugated. Alarmed by the expeditions of Bajazet, Sigismund, King of Hungary, sent ambassadors to demand an explanation of the conquests made so near his provinces. The Ottoman chief received the deputation in a hall adorned with Bulgarian arms and trophies, and he deigned no other answer than to point to the bows and arrows suspended against the walls, as a proof of his right to the possession of Bulgaria (1394). The same year, Bajazet, proud of his success, dropped the title of Emir and assumed that of Sultan.

Persuaded that war with Bajazet was inevitable, Sigismund endeavored to strengthen himself by soliciting an alliance with Charles VI., King of France. Having completed his preparations, he crossed the Danube and commenced operations by the siege of the little Nicopolis, which he took, notwithstanding the obstinate resistance of the garrison. However, the cause of Sigismund, the son and brother of emperors of the East, concerned the Church and Europe. At the first news of his danger, a crowd of adventurers from Italy, the bravest French and German knights, took up arms to oppose the common enemy of the Christian name. Early in the spring, Charles VI. sent to this new crusade about eight thousand mercenary troops and a body of a thousand knights. These various bands were under the nominal command of the Count of Nevers, afterwards known as John the Fearless, intrepid son of Philip the Bold, Duke of Burgundy. This prince, only twenty-two years of age, and without experience of war, was under the direction of the Count d' Eu, Constable of France, who was to command the army in the name of the young captain. The most illustrious persons were eager to share in the glory of the holy war. Among the nobles of high rank were the Counts de Bar and de la Marche, cousins of the King, Philip of Artois, the Admiral John de Vienne, the Sire de Coucy, Marshal Boucicaut, the Sire de Saimpy, Guy de Tremouille and the Lord de Saint Pol. On their passage through Germany these French noblemen were joined by Philibert de Naillac, grand master of St. John; Frederic of Hohenzollern, grand prior of the

Teutonic knights, and the Bavarian Schilterberg, the historian of the expedition. Valakian troops, under the command of their Prince, Myrtsche, helped to swell the army of the King of Hungary.

The auxiliaries having traversed Bavaria and Austria, joined Sigismund at Buda. At the sight of so many brave warriors, the king, assured of success, exclaimed: "Why should we fear the Turks? Should the heaven fall, we have lances enough to bear it up." The Christian army, sixty thousand strong, crossed the Danube, entered Bulgaria, took several cities, massacred the inhabitants without showing mercy to any, and laid siege to Nicopolis, an important city defended by a valiant garrison, to which Bajazet could soon send aid. After useless efforts to take it by assault, the besiegers, who were not provided with cannon, determined to reduce it by famine. Full of confidence in the superiority of their numbers, the allies indulged in every kind of pleasure, and spoke of the Sultan only in terms of contempt. They doubted that he would have the courage to cross the Bosphorus and attack them. But at the very moment they were abandoning themselves to a false security, the enemy was approaching.

Whilst the chief of the garrison of Nicopolis held the Christian army at bay under the walls of Nicopolis by a heroic defense, Bajazet had made his plans. A rapid march, skilfully concealed from the knowledge of the allies, brought his army within a short distance of their camp, in which there was neither discipline nor order. Warned of the approach of the enemy by some marauders who had been put to flight by the Turks, they raised the siege, and had the imprudent barbarity to massacre all the prisoners whom they held on parole. As soon as the Arabs, the vanguard of the enemy, covered the plain, the impetuous Count of Nevers demanded for the French cavalry the post of honor in the combat. King Sigismund, who had learned by sad experience the manner of fighting the Turks, begged the crusaders to place his Hungarians in the front, and thus oppose light-armed troops to light-armed, and reserve the flower of the army to meet the attack of the Janizaries and Spahis. But the French cavaliers would not, for a moment, entertain the proposition, declaring that they would never give way to the Hungarian infantry; and they rushed headlong to the contest (22d September, 1396). The Turkish infantry was shattered by the impetuous onslaught of the Count of Nevers and his valiant companions. Even the Janizaries were unable to resist this band of warriors. Ten thousand of their number had fallen on the field, and the remainder were retreating to the rear of the Spahis, when the French precipitated themselves upon this second corps and routed them. Urged on by their impetuous valor and no longer listening to the dictates of prudence, they pursued the fugitives without observing any order, until they reached the summit of a hill. What was their consternation when they saw themselves confronted by forty thousand of the élite of the troops of Bajazet! To surprise succeeded a panic terror, and they fled in frightful disorder. The knights alone resisted, and fought with the courage of despair. Surrounded on all sides by the cavalry, who were animated by the presence of the Sultan, the greater part found a glorious death by the sword of the enemy. The Count of Nevers and twenty-four of the principal nobles were made prisoners by the Turks.

The Hungarians had been drawn up in battle array at a very short distance behind the French. Stephen Lankovich commanded the left wing, and Prince Myrtsche the right wing, composed of Wallachians. No sooner did they behold the French retreating in disorder before the Ottomans, than both wings fled disgracefully, notwithstanding all the efforts of Sigismund to rally them. The Bavarians and Styrians bore the brunt of the battle. Being reinforced by some of the fugitive French, they rushed upon the troops of the Sultan and restored the battle. They had already driven back the Janizaries, and spread terror throughout the ranks of the Spahis, when the arrival of the Prince of Servia, ally of Bajazet, with a body of five thousand men, decided the victory, which had been held in the balance by their prodigies of valor. The largest number fell in defending the standard of Sigismund. The king himself, forced from the spot by the Archbishop of Grau and Stephen of Kanischa, his brother, reluctantly left the field of battle strewn with bodies of the Styrian and Bavarian knights; accompanied by a few brave companions, he cast himself into a small boat and rowed to the allied fleet of Venice and Rhodes, which was anchored at the mouth of the Danube. Thence he went to Constantinople, and by a circuitous route returned to his exhausted states.

Bajazet, victorious over the confederate army, encamped before Nicopolis, and the following day visited the field where the intrepid soldiers had so bravely contended with him. At the sight of the multitude of dead bodies of the Turks which strewed the plain, the number of which is estimated by some historians to have been over sixty thousand, he shed tears of rage, and swore to avenge in Christian blood the Mussulman warriors who had fallen under the sword of the enemy. He, consequently, ordered all the prisoners to be brought before him the following day. More than ten thousand were dragged into his presence, with ropes around their necks and their hands tied behind their backs. He consented to spare the Count of Nevers and twenty-four of the principal lords, among whom were the Count de la Marche, the Constable d'Eu, the Marshal Boucicaut, the Sires de Coucy, and Guy de Tremouille, expecting to obtain for them a heavy ransom; but he obliged them to witness the horrible expiation he had determined to exact in honor of the memory of his faithful Ottomans. The savage Sultan ordered a general massacre. Some of the unfortunate prisoners were beheaded, others beaten to death with clubs. The carnage continued without interruption from sunrise until four o'clock in the afternoon. It ceased then only at the supplication of the nobles of the empire, who, overcome by the frightful spectacle, threw themselves on their knees before Bajazet, and implored his mercy. The tyrant's thirst for vengeance was momentarily appeased by the blood of so many Christians, and he allowed the remainder to remain in the hands of those who had made them prisoners. The Count de Nevers and his twenty-four companions were loaded with chains and sent to the tower of Gallipoli.

The King of France and other princes united with Sigismund to send rich presents to the Sultan, in order to hasten the liberation of the French cavaliers. After the delay rendered necessary by the distance, Bajazet accepted two hundred thousand ducats for the ransom of the heir of Burgundy and the barons who were still alive. When the ransom, the amount of which had been doubled by incidental expenses, was paid, the Sultan restored to liberty the Count de Nevers, saying to him: "I free you from your oath never to bear arms against me; I conjure you, on the contrary, to resume them as soon as possible, and to bring hither all the forces of Christendom. You cannot do me a greater favor than to give me another opportunity of acquiring glory." Before the departure of the foreign captives, Bajazet received them at his Court, and entertained them with a falcon hunt. He astonished them by the magnificence of his suite, which was composed of seven thousand falconers and six thousand men serving his dogs.

The defeat of the Christians before the walls of Nicopolis was followed by an incursion of the Turks into the countries situated between the Save and the Drave. They devastated the fields of the ancient Sismium, but learning from his late victory not to attack the Europeans without sufficient preparation, Bajazet turned his arms against the Greeks, on whose territories his triumphs had been obtained without difficulty, and whom God seemed to abandon to his revenge. He summoned the Emperor to appear before him, to perform his duties as a vassal. Furious at a refusal, which he did not anticipate, he ordered his vizir to resume the siege of Constantinople, which had been interrupted by the expedition of the King of Hungary and his allies. Not satisfied with attacking the metropolis of the Christians of the East, he directed Timour-Tasch to extend the frontiers of the Ottoman empire to the north and east of Asia. Whilst this skillful lieutenant planted his victorious standard on the banks of the Euphrates, the Sultan, at the head of fifty-six thousand Mussulmans, fell like a thunderbolt upon Greece, subjugated, without opposition, the principal cities of Thessaly, penetrated through the pass of Thermopylæ, conquered Phocis, and left to two of his generals the acquisition of Peloponnesus (1367).

Obedient to the instructions of their barbarian sovereign, these two generals devastated the environs of Modon and Coron, and spared not the Greeks. The Prince of Sparta, Theodore Palæologus, animated by the most generous sentiments, sacrificed himself for the good of Christendom, and ceded his city to Philibert de Naillac, grand master of the Knights of Rhodes. The inhabitants, who found it impossible to divest themselves of their hatred against the West, opposed in the most violent manner the designs of Theodore. When the knights arrived to take possession of the city, these degenerate Spartans attacked them with stones and clubs, and desisted only at the command of their bishop. They clung to their name of Greek, and preferred death under this name to life under the protection of the Latins. In the meantime, the Mussulmans occupied Argos, plundered it and transported into Asia thirty thousand of its inhabitants, supplying their place by a colony of Ottomans.

Reduced to the last extremity, and shut up within his capital, the emperor was destitute of means to hire troops to defend it. The great prince of Moscow, Vassali, learning the deplorable condition of the emperor, sent him a large sum of money by the monk Osliebia, and induced all the Russian princes to follow his example. These presents were received at Constantinople with transports of joy and gratitude by the emperor, the Patriarch, and the people.

Andronicus the elder, brother of Manuel, who had been deprived of sight by the barbarous Amurat, and who had abdicated after usurping the crown, left at his death in the service of the Turks a son named John Selymbia. To create additional difficulties for Manuel, the Sultan pretended to consider this prince as the legitimate sovereign of Constantinople, and urged him to assert his rights to the throne. He had no doubt of the readiness of his protégé to do his bidding, and if we may rely upon the assertions of the historian Ducas, he had forced from him the promise to cede Constantinople in exchange for the Morea. He even sent to the emperor a message couched in these terms: "Resign the crown to the rightful heir, from whom you have usurped it, and I will immediately lay down my arms and grant peace to the city." Struggling with the misery which pervaded his capital, with the demands of Bajazet, and the clamors of the friends of John, who reproached him with ruining the empire by his ambition and establishing his own domination by the destruction of his country, Manuel prudently resolved to share the throne with his nephew. Accordingly he received him in his palace, and promised the sultan to present himself at the *Porte* whenever his services should be required (1399).

While such was the sad state of affairs in the East, Charles VI., King of France, had obstinately refused the petition of his brother, the Duke of Orleans, to confide to him the command of a new crusade. He was, however, persuaded to send six hundred men-at-arms and eight hundred regular troops under the brave Boucicaut to the shores of the Bosphorus.

The Marshal had great difficulty in penetrating to Constantinople. When he undertook to cross the Hellespont, his little fleet was opposed by seventeen well-armed Mussulman galleys, which were waiting at Gallipoli to intercept his passage. Notwithstanding the inferiority of his forces, Boucicaut repulsed the assailants, put them to flight, arrived in a few days before Galata, and by relieving that city saved Constantinople. The Greeks welcomed him as a guardian angel, loaded him with honors, and appointed him Grand Constable of the Greek empire.

The arrival of the Marshal, whose zeal was increased by the remembrance of his captivity and the desire of revenge, compelled Bajazet to raise the siege of Constantinople. Boucicaut's attacks upon several fortresses of Europe and Asia were crowned with success, but he failed in taking Nicomedia.

The Ottomans, who had at first retreated to some distance, soon reappeared in greater numbers. Having remained a year, the Marshal determined to abandon a country where he could no longer protect his troops, and in which they were unable to obtain a sufficient support. He induced Manuel to accompany him to France, where he promised that he would himself beg both men and money to aid his cause, assuring him that his presence would rouse the knights of the West and awaken their piety to engage in a crusade. The emperor, trusting to these assurances, confided the government of the empire to his nephew, and embarked for Peloponnesus. His brother Theodore, Despot of Lacedemon, strongly disapproved of his design, predicting that his journey would be as fruitless as the one which had been formerly undertaken for the same purpose. He represented the imprudence of which he was guilty in placing the government of the empire in the hands of a young prince without experience, and whose interests were opposed to his own.

Manuel was not moved by the wise remonstrances of his brother. Having left his wife and two young children, John and Theodore, at Modon, he set out for Italy. Instead of praising the success of his vassal, thus become master of Constantinople, the sultan hastened to recall him to a sense of his duty, and in accordance with the wish of his suzerain, John Palæologus allowed a mosque to be built in the city, instituted a court of justice, and appointed a cadi to decide in their own language upon cases in which Mussulmen were concerned.

No beneficial results attended the journey of Manuel through the States of the West. This prince did not comprehend the age; Europe was no longer in the times of Godfrey de Bouillon and St. Bernard, nor even of Louis IX. Other interests had obtained the ascendency over the interests of religion, and Catholic Europe was about to abandon to the Ottoman power the empire of the degenerate Greeks. The heir of the Cæsars was received at Venice, Genoa and Florence with extraordinary magnificence, but his petitions for aid were unheeded. From Venice he went to Padua and Pavia. The Duke of Milan, John Galeas, furnished him with money, horses and guides to enable him to appear with becoming dignity at the court of France, where he was expected. He even protested that he was willing to march in person to the relief of Constantinople, if the other princes would unite with him in the expedition.

Charles VI., who considered the sojourn of a Greek emperor in his states as a glorious event of his reign, had given orders that he should be received with all the honors due his rank. As soon as the guest, so impatiently desired, touched the soil of France, the officers of the king met him, and from that time defrayed all expenses. In every city through which he passed the people thronged the way and filled the air with their joyous acclamations. A cavalcade composed of two thousand of the wealthiest citizens of Paris went as far as Charenton to escort him thence to the city. At the gates of the capital, he was welcomed by the Chancellor, the Parliament and three Cardinals. Following them appeared Charles VI., accompanied by the princes of the blood and a numerous retinue of dukes, counts and courtiers, magnificently attired. The successor of Constantine was presented with a superb white horse and clothed in a mantle of white silk. Although not tall, Manuel was graceful and dignified. His expression of countenance was very agreeable; the long beard which covered his chin and the white hair which fell upon his shoulders, inspired interest and respect. The party proceeded to the royal palace, where a sumptuous banquet had been prepared.

Manuel was lodged at the Louvre; Charles VI. assigned him from his own treasures a sum sufficient to maintain a state befitting the imperial dignity. This monarch lost no opportunity to impress the Greeks with a high idea of his wealth and power. Balls and entertainments succeeded each other daily, and the French endeavored, by varying the pleasures of the hunt and the table, to divert the attention of their illustrious guest from his sorrows. They granted him a private chapel for his use, and the Parisians remarked with surprise the language, ceremonies and vestments of the Greek clergy. The emperor was not long in perceiving that he had nothing to expect from France. The unfortunate Charles VI. enjoyed the use of reason only for short intervals, and when he relapsed into a state of madness, his brother, the Duke of Orleans, and his uncle, Philip the Bold, were contending for the reins of government. This disastrous rivalry shortly broke out into civil war. The former, young and impetuous, of graceful and attractive manners, and agreeable in conversation, gave himself up to every kind of pleasure. The latter, the father of the Count de Nevers, strove to maintain a decided superiority over all the princes of the blood. Extensive domains, military reputation, talents, wealth, all seemed combined to add to the glory of the House of Burgundy. The intrepid John de Nevers was eager to efface the disgrace of Nicopolis by undertaking another expedition; but his father, profiting by the experience of the former fruitless attempt, refused to furnish the necessary means.

A few months after his arrival in Paris, the emperor determined to go to England to solicit aid, as Charles VI. was at that time afflicted with an attack of insanity. At Canterbury he was welcomed with great honor by the monks of St. Augustine. King Henry IV., accompanied by a numerous suite and many of the nobles, received the Greek monarch at Blackheath, and entertained him several days in his capital. But England was even less disposed than France to enter upon a war against the infidels. That very year the legitimate sovereign, Richard II., had been dethroned and put to death by the ambitious usurper, Henry of Lancaster. A prey to anxiety and remorse, Henry dared not weaken his forces by a foreign expedition, when his own subjects were actually disposed to revolt. He, therefore, limited his sympathy to expressions of compassion for the Greek emperor, and to bestowing upon him rich presents.

In the month of February of the following year, Manuel returned to France, as the king was restored to health. As to Bajazet, he had no fear of the imperial beggar who was striving to raise up enemies against him among the Christian princes, and seeking by foreign hands to arrest the downfall of his empire. He had planted Islamism in the heart of Constantinople; the iman prayed in his mosque, the cadi presided over his tribunal. The sultan at this time resided at Brusa (Prusa), the seat of his tyrannical rule. The tree of his fortune, elevating its trunk and spreading out its branches, afforded him daily an abundance of the most delicious fruits to contribute to his pleasures. No enjoyment was wanting to him: animals of wonderful forms, precious metals—in a word, all that God has created to gratify the sight, were found in his palace. The Greeks, Wallachians, Albanians, Hungarians, Saxons, Bulgarians and Latins vied with each other in presenting to him young captives, who at the given signal came into his presence to sing in their own native tongue. His slaves were the obedient ministers of his will. Thus Bajazet was giving himself up to the pleasures of his court at Brusa, awaiting the favorable moment to crush entirely the wreck of the Greek empire, when his life of ease was interrupted and his pride alarmed by an Eastern chief.

The head of one of the tribes of the dismembered empire of Gengis-Khan, Timour, surnamed *Lend*, or the *Lame*, called by Western historians Tamerlane, being deprived of his inheritance in his infancy by an unjust conqueror, grew up in obscurity amid the forests of upper Asia. When he was strong enough to avenge his wrongs, he placed himself at the head of a few wandering Tartars, whose numbers gradually increased; he accustomed them to military exercises, and enriched them by pillage.

Having gained a great victory before the walls of Samarcand, the ambitious Timour founded a principality of which this city was the centre; he was afterwards proclaimed Saheb-Keran (master of the world), in a *couroultai* or national diet (1370). Invested with supreme authority, wearing a golden crown, he made a solemn oath in presence of his emirs kneeling around him, to combat all the princes of the earth. He spent one year in restoring order in Samarcand, and then departed on his career of conquest.

Timour crossed the Sihoum (Oxus), invaded and subjugated Kashgar, destroyed the capital of Kharism, whose inhabitants he put to the sword, subdued the east coast of the Caspian Sea and a large portion of Persia. He established on his throne the fugitive prince, Toktamisch, who had sought refuge at his court. But after a reign of ten years, the new khan, forgetting his obligations to his powerful benefactor, revolted against him. Tamerlane entered his dominions, dispersed his numerous army, and compelled him to fly. Prudence and ambition recalled him from the pursuit of Toktamisch towards the south. He reduced the city of Azof to ashes, and condemned to death or slavery all the Christians who fell into his hands. He treated in like manner the cities of Astrachan and Serai.

After an expedition of five years, the conqueror returned to Samarcand with an immense booty. He was met on the banks of the Oxus by the princesses of his household and the wives of his sons, who, according to the custom of the Tartars, poured over his head pieces of gold and precious stones, and presented him with a thousand horses, richly caparisoned, and a thousand mules. He visited Kesh, the second capital of his empire, of which his ancestors had been hereditary chiefs, and upon which he had bestowed the name of Temple of Science and Civilization. At Samarcand he gave his army time to recruit from the fatigues of war. But his vigorous old age could not long endure an inactive life, and the indomitable *destroyer* undertook the conquest of Hindoostan, the distant definitive aim of all conquerors of the world. Unheeding the murmurs of his emirs, who were wearied of long continued war, the great khan put himself at the head of his innumerable squadrons. In vain the Scapouch took refuge in their mountains, situated between the Gihon and the Indus—they were subjugated or exterminated; snows, torrents, precipices, nothing could impede his rapid march (1398). Afghanistan was traversed in six months, the Indus crossed, and desolation and terror spread over the land. There had not yet been a heavy battle, and already the Tartar army held a hundred thousand prisoners. But these innocent victims might, by their numbers, prevent the success of the first engagement with the enemy; so they were slaughtered by Timour's order in the space of one hour.

Having arrived before Delhi, a large and flourishing city, the residence of the Sultan Mahmoud, whose weakness was well known to him, he was unwilling to waste the time required for a siege. He, therefore, dexterously concealed the amount of his forces, enticed the sultan into the open field; his army was accompanied by a hundred and twenty elephants. As soon as the Moguls had put to flight these clumsy animals, the Indians disappeared without striking a blow. The savage invader made his triumphal entrance into the capital of Hindoostan, and disgraced the rejoicings of victory by ordering the sack of the city and a general massacre. Nearly all the inhabitants, animated by the courage of despair, set fire to their own houses, and perished in the flames. At other places on their route, the devastating hordes renewed these scenes of desolation and carnage, burning the men alive and leading captive the women and children. Where they passed, nothing remained of the strongest cities but a heap of ashes. The Ganges opposed in vain its waves to the impetuosity of Timour. He pushed on to the scource of this river, exterminating everywhere, in honor of Mahomet, all the fire-worshippers, destroying their cities and inundating the ruins with human blood. He then marched along the frontiers of the wonderful vale of Cashmere, where the prince and a number of Indian chiefs went to prostrate themselves at his feet. Two years had sufficed to secure these conquests, and the invincible Timour returned to Samarcand, where, to immortalize their successful expedition, he erected a magnificent mosque by the labor of several thousand Indian and Persian workmen, whom he had forced to accompany him.

The conquered people, however, did not wear the yoke patiently. Couriers inform the victor that Georgia, Bagdad and Diarbekir have risen in revolt. He returns immediately, subdues the rebels, and leaves traces of his devastating march. Tamerlane is also animated by a zeal for proselytism; he puts to death by frightful tortures all who refuse to embrace the religion of the prophet.

His ambition was not satiated by the conquest of the States of Asia. After reposing seven months at Samarcand, he set out upon an expedition to the West. His first blows were aimed against the Christians of Georgia, whose defences were their mountains, their fortresses, and the severe cold of the winter: but Tamerlane triumphed over every obstacle; he forced the enemy from their mountain retreats, took Tiflis, the capital of the country, and other important places (1400). He was passing the summer in the beautiful plain of Karabagh, when the Seljonkian emirs, despoiled by Bajazet of Anatolia, took refuge in his camp and implored his protection. Convinced that a mere remonstrance from him would prove efficacious, Tamerlane sent ambassadors to the haughty Ottoman, to carry the following message: "The great Tamerlane tells you by the mouth of his servants: You have no right to take what belongs to others, and to aggrandize yourself by acts of injustice. Be contented with that portion which God has permitted you to conquer from the infidels; but you must restore those provinces which, like a thief, you have taken from other princes, and thus God will be propitious to you. If you refuse, I will avenge their wrongs."

Indignant at this insolent message, Bajazet was about to punish the envoys of the great khan; but he was persuaded to change his intention by prudent counsellors, who reminded him of the respect paid in the East to the character of an ambassador. He, however, cut off their beards, and sent them back with an insulting reply. "Go tell your master," he said, "that I am waiting for him, and let him come quickly." To prove to Tamerlane how completely he despised his menaces, he conducted his army into Armenia, took Erzendjan, and returned to Brusa. Then, as if to show that he also had the right to command slaves as a master, he summoned the nephew of Manuel to surrender his capital. "I elevated you to the throne of this city," wrote the sultan, "that I might add it to my empire; give it up, if you wish to preserve my friendship. I will bestow upon you any other province you may desire; if you refuse, I call God and the prophet to witness that I will spare no one, but exterminate all." The Byzantines, undisturbed by the menaces of a new siege, collected a large quantity of provisions, and, full of Christian confidence and noble pride, they answered the ambassador: "Say to your master that, weak as we are, we know no power to save us but God, who can give us strength, and who can humble the strongest of our enemies. Let the sultan do what he wills." The success of Tamerlane prevented Bajazet from accomplishing his purpose, and retarded the fall of Constantinople.

Upon receiving an account of the insult offered him in the person of his deputies, the great khan unfurled his banner and entered the Ottoman territory the 22d August, 1400. His first attack was upon Sirvas, the ancient Sebaste, one of the strongest and most populous cities of Asia. Art was united with nature to render it impregnable. Summoned in vain to open its gates, it was unable, notwithstanding its advantages, to avoid the catastrophe prepared for it by the anger of the Tartar emperor. It was defended on three sides by a ditch filled with water; the assailants commenced digging at the distance of a mile on the west, in order, by an underground passage, to reach the foundations of the ramparts and undermine them without being discovered. After the work was completed, Tamerlane sent a second summons, which the inhabitants received with insults. Immediately a large portion of the walls crumbled with a loud noise, and the Moguls, penetrating the city, inflicted upon it all the horrors of pillage. Never had Tamerlane carried his ferocity to a greater extent. He caused a large pit to be excavated like a tomb, and ordered all the inhabitants who had survived the carnage to be cast into it, their bodies being first bent and their heads tied by ropes between their legs. Upon the top were placed planks, over which earth was thrown, that the unfortunate victims might die by a slow agony. One of the sons of Bajazet, Ertroghul, paid for his heroic resistance with his life. The conqueror ordered him to be executed.

The horrible vengeance of Tamerlane and the death of his most valiant son, filled the Ottoman sultan with the deepest grief. Forced by this frightful news to withdraw from Constantinople and thus grant a momentary repose to Palæologus, Bajazet crossed into Asia. But ere he had reached the eastern frontier of his empire, the Tartar wave had rolled far to the south, marking its path with desolation. The conqueror, satisfied with giving this first lesson to his new enemy, had returned to

Syria to chastise the sultan of the Mameluks, the weak Pharega, whose father had defied him and arrested his ambassadors. Instead of defending themselves within the walls of their fortress, the Syrians, aided by an army from Egypt, advanced to meet the Tartars in the open field, and were crushed by the impetuous squadrons of Tamerlane. The conqueror pursued the fugitives into the city over heaps of dead, sacked it and massacred the inhabitants without regard to sex or age. Tamerlane remained two days in the citadel, that from its height he might contemplate the work of destruction. Thence he went to the governor's palace and celebrated his victory by a magnificent banquet. Whilst the vast halls resounded with joyous shouts of the revellers, blood was flowing in the streets of Aleppo, and cries of terror mingled with the groans of the dying, filled the air. Before he departed a monument composed of the heads of the conquered was erected in his honor.

The fall of Aleppo was followed in quick succession by that of Hama, Hems, and other fortified towns of Syria. Tamerlane next occupied Balbeck, a populous city, which furnished his army with an ample supply of provisions, and thence he marched against Damascus. The inhabitants defended themselves most valiantly, and the great khan, perceiving that they could hold him in check for a long time, offered to raise the siege if they would redeem their city from pillage by the payment of a million pieces of gold. They consented to the conditions, relying upon his faith. But Tamerlane, one day expressed to his counsellors his great indignation against the inhabitants because they had formerly ill-treated the prophets, particularly Ali and his son Hosein. The religious fervor of the conqueror for Ali and Hosein, against the descendants of the first partisans of Moawia and Yezid, had such influence over the members of the council, and still more over the army, that notwithstanding the capitulation and the payment of the required ransom, they entered the city sword in hand, and in a few moments Damascus was in flames. Tamerlane dispatched an emir with directions to save, if possible, the most ancient master-piece of Saracen architecture, the grand mosque of the Ommiades, but he found the metal which covered the roof flowing in molten streams.

Obliged by the losses and fatigues of this campaign to renounce the conquest of Egypt and Palestine, the chief of the Moguls retraced his steps, delivered Aleppo to the flames, crossed the Euphrates and besieged Bagdad, which was obstinately defended by its governor. He, however, obtained possession of it during the summer, exterminated all the inhabitants, and of this ancient capital of Islamism, once so flourishing, he spared only the mosques, the schools, and the convents; a pyramid of ninety thousand human heads arose above the ruins of Bagdad as a monument of the barbarity of the conqueror.

The arrival of Tamerlane had restored the hope of life to the Greeks; the day of chastisement had come for Bajazet. Seeing that his remonstrances produced no effect, and irritated by the insulting messages of the sultan, the great khan entered Anatola a second time at the head of eight hundred thousand barbarians, and approached Angora, taking at the same time all the precautions dictated by prudence. To meet this army, which the Byzantines compared to that of Xexes, Bajazet could bring only a hundred and twenty thousand Tartars and ten thousand Servians. He selected for his army a field through which ran a river, whence he might draw the water necessary for his troops. When, on the contrary, he saw Tamerlane encamped on a dry, arid plain, he affected a profound contempt for him, and ordered a general hunt for that and the two following days on the elevated plateaus of the environs. After this foolish excursion of three days, under a burning sun, in which five thousand of his soldiers perished from fatigue and thirst, he returned to his camp; he found it occupied by the Moguls. To increase his difficulties, the spring from which the water flowed had been so filled by the enemy that it was nearly dried up.

The two great rulers of the East were now face to face; but their chances of victory were by no means equal. In addition to superiority of numbers, two circumstances of good omen, according to the ideas of the time, presaged success to the arms of Tamerlane: first, before his departure from his capital, a grandson had been born to him, and during the festivities in honor of that event gold pieces and pearls had been poured over his head; next, a fiery comet of extraordinary size had appeared in the heavens, and moving from the West to the East. Its brilliancy was so great as to eclipse that of the stars; its rays of uncommon length flamed like lances turned towards the East. For more than three months this meteor shone over the whole earth. The nations, from the Indus and the Ganges to the Rhine and the Tagus, were terrified. The Greeks considered it a prediction of bloody battles in the East; to the astrologers and Tamerlane's companions in arms it announced certain victory to them in the regions of the West.

This first check experienced by Bajazet did not diminish his confidence. His vizier, Ali Pasha, and his son, Ibrahim, advised him to avoid a pitched battle, and to exhaust his enemy slowly by skirmishes in the mountains, defiles and woods; but he rejected their prudent counsel. His army, discontented with his extreme severity, and being, moreover, badly paid, broke out into murmurs; this was particularly the case with the auxiliaries. The parsimonious sultan was unwilling to open his own treasures, by which he might have appeased the troops and purchased a victory of which he felt secure without making the sacrifice. The obstinacy and blindness of Bajazet and the disaffection of the soldiery destroyed all the hopes of the generals of conquering the innumerable army of the Moguls.

In a vast plain situated to the northeast of Angora, on the very ground where Pompey had formerly defeated Mithridates, the Ottomans and Tartars were drawn up in battle array; the former commanded by the sultan, the latter by the emperor. The different divisions were under the orders of princes, sons and grandsons of the two sovereigns, and of the most valiant generals of Europe and Asia. Tamerlane thus harangued his army: "Invincible troops, wall of defence harder than diamond, you know the glorious exploits by which our ancestors rendered themselves famous, not only in the East, our birthplace, but also in Europe and Africa —I may say throughout the universe. You are not ignorant of the celebrated expeditions of Xerxes and Artaxerxes against the Greeks, those gods and demigods, with whom the Turks can no more compare than grasshoppers with lions. It is not to awaken your courage that I recall these exploits, for the prey is already in our grasp; but to urge you not to let your enemies escape, to conduct them alive to your own country, to show them to our children, and to teach them never again to provoke our wrath. Let the two wings approach at each end, so as to form a circle inclosing the enemy in the centre." At six o'clock in the morning the two wings commenced the movement as directed, and surrounded the plain.

Seeing the soldiers of the great khan executing this evolution in profound silence, Bajazet laughed and ridiculed the men who seemed to him to be cowards because they uttered no cry. The signal being given, the Ottomans moved to the sound of drums and the war-cry *Allah!* At the commencement of the action, a Seljoukian chief, who was serving unwillingly under the banner of the sultan, perceiving Aidin, his former prince, in the ranks of the enemy, deserted with five hundred men. In an instant he was followed by the contingents of Mentesche, Saronkan and Caramania, and by the Tartars, who had been won over by the letters and secret emissaries of Tamerlane. Bajazet's fears were aroused when he beheld the multitude of Moguls, deploying in a semi-circle, advance their two wings on the two sides of the Ottoman army, so as to meet in its rear. Stephen V., son of Lazarus and brother-in-law of the sultan, furious at the perfidy of the deserters, commenced the attack with incredible valor at the head of five thousand Servians, broke the ranks of the enemy and cut a passage for himself. A second attack as furious as the first again forced a way through, notwithstanding the depth of the line. But Stephen, approaching Bajazet, advised him to fly; he saw the most heroic efforts would be useless against so numerous a host. At the same moment he noticed a body of Servians seize Soliman, the eldest son of the sultan; opening a way for themselves a third time with irresistible rapidity, they fled towards the west to gain the sea.

Abandoned by his auxiliaries and his own troops, by his viziers and emirs, Bajazet still determined to make a stand; he seized an eminence where resistance might be successful, and defended it with ten thousand Janizaries. But the Mogul hordes could divide with impunity, and attack all sides at the same moment. Some pursued the Servians on the route to Brusa; a second body cut to pieces the principal corps of the Ottomans, and a third precipitated themselves upon the Janizaries. These intrepid soldiers defended themselves with unexampled courage. Nearly all of them fell, overpowered by the heat, consumed by thirst, exhausted by fatigue, or pierced by the sword of the enemy. Bajazet, mounted on an Arab steed, was left alone above the heap of his slaughtered guards. "Descend," cried out a Tartar to him, "the Khan Tamerlane requires your presence." The haughty sultan obeyed, and mounted a small horse which the Moguls had in readiness to conduct him to their master. His son, Musa, and some of his principal emirs, were likewise made prisoners (20 July, 1402).

When Bajazet was introduced, Tamerlane, certain of the victory, affected to despise him, and continued a game of chess with his son Schabroch. The Moguls bade their illustrious captive stand at the threshold of the imperial tent, and after a burst of joyous acclamations in honor of their chief, they said to him: "Behold Bajazet, the prince of the Turks, is in your power; we have brought him to your presence loaded with chains." The great khan remained bending over his game, as if he had not heard their words. Their repeated cries at last attracted his attention. "You are then the prince who threatened us if we refused to make war against him," he said, regarding Bajazet. "I am he," replied the sultan, "but it does not become you to despise the conquered; learn to use your power with moderation." The pride of the conqueror was not offended by the pride of the vanquished. The emperor, noticing that his prisoner was overpowered by the heat and covered with dust, seated him by his side, and assured him in the kindest terms, in the name of God and his people, that he need have no fear for his life, and that God alone, who had united them, should separate his soul from his body.

The sultan afterwards retired to one of the three magnificent tents assigned for his use by Tamerlane, that he might repose after so fatiguing a battle;

he requested information of his sons, and asked for the consolation of their company. Messengers were dispatched in every direction, but they discovered only the prince Musa. The guards placed around Bajazet and his son under the orders of Hasan Beslas, one of the highest Tartar emirs and a relative of the sultan, acquitted themselves of their charge with as much respect as vigilance. The kindness extended to the sultan inspired him with the hope of being able to make his escape. Mahomet, his third son, who had survived the bloody defeat of Angora, resolved to deliver his father, who was allowed considerable liberty. Turkish miners entered the Mogul camp during the night, and commenced from an adjoining tent to dig a subterranean passage conducting to the one occupied by Bajazet. The work was already advanced, and the noble captive was cherishing the hope of being shortly restored to liberty, when a new division of guards sent to relieve those who had been upon duty, discovered the work and gave the alarm. They hastened to the tent of the sultan and found him with Khodja-Firouy, his faithful servant, prepared to attempt an escape. Mahomet and the miners made good their retreat. Irritated by this effort of his prisoner, Tamerlane overwhelmed him with reproaches and threats, and ordered Khodja-Firouy to be executed as the instigator of the enterprise. From that day Bajazet was closely confined, the number of his guards was increased, and during the night he was chained hand and foot. From this extreme severity arose the story of the iron cage, which the credulous accepted without any reasonable foundation.

The disastrous day of Angora annihilated the work of Amurat and Bajazet. A grandson of the conqueror marched against Brusa, and its capture was marked by all the horrors which signalized the conquests of those savage hordes, and by the pillage of the rich treasures of the first capital of the Ottoman sultans. The great khan next traversed Asia Minor, and reinstated in their principalities the Seljoukian emirs, in whose names he had combatted Bajazet. Of the five sons of the sultan, Musa, the second, shared his captivity; the youngest, Mustapha, had disappeared. To secure the ruin of the empire, Tamerlane divided between the other three all the dominions of their father which he had not occupied himself; Soliman received the investiture of the Ottoman possessions in Europe; Isa, a part of Anatola, and Mahomet, the city of Amasia.

All historians, Byzantine as well as Ottoman, agree that the cruelties exercised by the ferocious Tamerlane in his campaign of Asia Minor surpassed all the scenes of carnage which had hitherto been witnessed. Weary of victory and satiated with blood, this merciless exterminator of nations was on his way to Samarcand, when the unfortunate Bajazet died of an attack of apoplexy at Akshehr, the Antioch of Pisidia, about nine months after his defeat (1404). On receiving the news of this premature death, Tamerlane repeated the words of the Koran: "We belong to God, and we return to Him." It is said that he shed tears over the tomb of the sultan, his enemy, and permitted Musa to convey with pomp the body of his father to the mausoleum he had constructed at Brusa. He granted his liberty to Musa, and the right to claim a portion of the inheritance from his brothers; he clothed him with a mantle of honor, presented him a magnificent girdle, a sabre, and a quiver enriched with precious stones.

After having completed the conquest of Georgia, passed the winter on the banks of the Araxa, and settled disturbances in Persia, Tamerlane re-entered Samarcand for the ninth time. During a short interval of repose, he displayed on the throne all the magnificence and authority of a rich and powerful monarch. He listened to the complaints of the people, and awarded punishments or recompenses according to the merits of the case. By the aid of the architects and artists made prisoners at the siege of Damascus, he embellished his residence with temples and palaces surpassing in beauty those which had been already erected in the Tartar capital. In the immense plain of Kanighul the great khan celebrated with extraordinary magnificence the nuptials of six princes, his grandsons. The ambassadors of all the sovereigns of Asia were present at the ceremony, and they placed at the feet of the emperor the richest and most costly presents. At the termination of these festivities, Tamerlane unfurled the imperial banner, and regardless of his age and the severity of the winter, he turned his steps toward China. Arriving at Otrar, where death awaited him, he was attacked by a burning fever, which was augmented by fatigue and the imprudent use of ice-water; he expired in the seventy-first year of his age, after a reign of thirty-six years, leaving behind him the reputation of having been the greatest destroyer of cities and nations whom the world had ever seen.

CHAPTER IV.

PEACE IN THE EMPIRE—MANUEL OPPOSES MUSTAPHA TO THE SULTAN AMURAT II.

Manuel, returning to Constantinople, banishes his nephew John to the island of Lemaos—Soliman makes an alliance with the Greek Emperor—Discord among the Mussulman Princes—Isa, conquered by his brother, Mahomet, disappears from the political scene—Soliman goes to Asia—Stratagem of Musa—Return of Soliman to Europe—Defeat of Musa—Soliman is deserted by his emirs—His death—Musa master of the Ottoman provinces of Europe—His cruel and despotic disposition—Musa's resentment against the Greeks—Ravage of Servia—Siege of Constantinople by Musa—Mahomet makes an alliance with Manuel—He is unfortunate in his defense of Constantinople, and crosses over to Asia—He returns to Europe—He pursues his brother—Death of Musa—Accession of Mahomet I.—Reception of the Greek ambassadors by the Sultan—Mahomet renews the treaty of peace with the Christian Princes—Marriage of Prince John with Anne of Russia—Death of this Princess—Baptism and death of a son of Bajazet—Second marriage of John with a daughter of the Marquis of Montferrat—Third marriage—Success of Mahomet in Asia—The imposter Mustapha—Interview of Mahomet with Manuel—Death of Mahomet I.—Amurat II. his successor—Mustapha restored to liberty—His success—His defeat—His death.

THE unexpected diversion of the Khan of Tartary had revived the courage of the Christians. Returning to Constantinople, after having uselessly exposed his griefs in the capitals of Europe, Manuel watched a favorable opportunity to resume the supreme authority. Upon receiving the news of the defeat of the Ottomans, by which Bajazet had been hurled like a star from heaven from the height of grandeur, he banished the Prince of Selymbria to the island of Lesbos, and remained sole sovereign. Soliman, having escaped the disaster of Angora, sought refuge at first at Brusa, but being pursued by the Tartars, he continued his flight, and went to Constantinople to implore the protection of the emperor. "I beg you," he said to him, "to be a father to me, and I will obey you as a submissive son; I ask only the government of Thrace and the other provinces which my ancestors possessed." Soliman afterwards promised to restore Thessalonica, the cities situated on the banks of the Strymon, the Morca, and the forts along the shore of the Propontis and the Euxine Sea. In order to cement more firmly his union with Manuel, he married the daughter of Theodore, the emperor's brother, leaving at the Byzantine court as hostages one of his young brothers and his sister Fatima.

Like a strong tree which has bent to the storm, the Ottoman empire recovered itself as soon as the tempest had passed, and we shall soon see it resuming its vigor, although the civil discords of the Mussulman princes threatened it with destruction. Mahomet, the youngest of the sultan's sons, commenced the struggle. Before his captivity, his father had confided to him the government of Amasia, which was the Turkish barrier against the Christians of Trebizond and Georgia, its citadel being considered impregnable by the Asiatics. In the course of his expeditions, the victor of Angora seems to have overlooked this angle of Anatola. Skilful and courageous, Mahomet was able to maintain his independence, and to drive from his province all the Mogul soldiery. After the death of Bajazet, he marched at the head of his troops to attack Isa, and dispossess him of Brusa, where he had fixed his residence. Overcome by the troops of Mahomet, Isa hastily left Asia, and sought an asylum at Constantinople, whilst the aggressor took possession of Brusa and Isnik. Having secured assistance from Soliman, Isa returned to Asia, but failed in an attempt to enter Brusa by surprise. Three subsequent defeats forced him to retreat to the mountainous parts of Caramania, where he disappeared, as his brother Mustapha had formerly done after the disastrous day of Ancyra.

When Isa had quitted the scene, attention was fixed upon Soliman, a brave and energetic prince, successful in war, uniting clemency to intrepidity, but intemperate and indolent. Up to this time he had remained a passive spectator of the war carried on by his two brothers in Asia; but roused from his apathy by the victories of Mahomet over Isa and the treason of Djourneïd, governor of Smyrna, he collected his troops, and marched upon Brusa, which threw open its gates to receive him. In the meantime, Djouneïd had leagued with the princes of Caramania and Kermian, and he soon found himself at the head of a large army. But being secretly warned of a plot of his allies to betray him to Soliman, he escaped from Ephesus during the night, went to the camp of this prince, and at early dawn presented himself before him with a rope around his neck, in the attitude of a repentant suppliant. "I acknowledge, my lord," he said, "that I am guilty and that I deserve death. Do with me as it pleases you." At the sight of the culprit thus humbling himself, Soliman was touched with compassion, and pardoned him. The defection of Djouneïd filled the allied army with consternation, and they disbanded in the utmost disorder. Soliman entered Ephesus in triumph, where he abandoned himself to intoxication and licentiousness.

In the meantime his vizier, Ali Pasha, had by stratagem rendered himself master of Angora, and successfully defended Brusa against the attack of Mahomet, obliging this prince to retreat to Amasia. But at this time Musa proposed to Mahomet to unite with him in combatting Soliman in the heart of his own states, and Mahomet crossed into Europe.

Obliged to abandon his project of the conquest of Asia by the powerful diversion of Musa in the provinces of Europe, Soliman crossed the Hellespont, and approached Constantinople to claim from his ally, the Greek emperor, the aid he had promised him. The first engagement between the two brothers took place in the vicinity of this city. Secretly won over by Byzantine emissaries, the troops of Stephen, Prince of Servia, a partisan of Musa, ranged themselves at the very commencement of the action under the standard of Soliman. Musa being defeated, retreated to the states of the Prince of Walachia; the conqueror retook Adrianople, where he was received amid the acclamations of the people, and was a second time acknowledged sultan of the Ottomans by all the Christian powers bordering on the empire.

Musa devoted himself to collecting a new army, whilst Soliman gave himself up to a life of pleasure in Adrianople. Manuel strove in vain to rouse him to take active measures against Musa; the prince was deaf to his remonstrances, and continued to pass his nights in orgies and his days in sleep. Suddenly Musa appeared with his army at the gates of Adrianople, and Soliman, who had been rendered by his excesses cruel, unjust and odious to his people, found himself almost alone at the moment of danger. Abandoned by the chiefs of his army who, with the exception of three, passed over to his brother, he fled towards Constantinople. The beauty of his horse and the magnificence of his apparel caused him to be recognized by the inhabitants of the village of Dougoundji, who had been cruelly treated by his soldiers. Five brothers, skilful knights and experienced archers, rode forward to meet him, animated perhaps only by the desire of seeing him. But the prince took his bow and shot the first, and then the second; the three others pierced him with their arrows and beheaded him (1410).

Having become by his brother's death absolute master of the Ottoman provinces in Europe, Musa proclaimed himself, immediately on his accession, the friend of the Servians and Greeks; but he soon exhibited a cruel and despotic disposition. He ordered the three murderers of Soliman to be taken to their own dwellings, all the inhabitants of the village, including women and children, to be shut up in their houses and burned alive, in expiation of the death of a prince, who ought not, he said, to have perished by the hands of slaves. He cherished a deep resentment against Manuel, his brother's former ally, and in an assembly of the nobles from Thrace, Macedonia and other provinces, who had come to do him homage, he betrayed his projects of vengeance. "You," he said, "who were formerly the friends and not the servants of my father, know how Asia was disturbed by the arms of Tamerlane, and how my father fell into his power. The emperor and the inhabitants of Constantinople enticed the Scythians, Persians and other foreign nations into our country. My brother, governing Thrace and the other provinces, which my father had possessed, forgot the sentiments of respect and piety which should have animated him towards his people, and God withdrew from him. He has placed in my hand the sword of the prophet, to exterminate the infidels and exalt the faithful. It is not just that Constantinople should possess so many cities, particularly Thessalonica, which was acquired by my father with much labor, and where he converted the temples of idols into temples of God and his prophet. If it pleases God, I will subjugate the mother of cities, and of the churches therein contained I will make houses of God and his prophet."

The assembly applauded the discourse as though it were an oracle proceeding from the very mouth of the Divinity. Musa, to avenge the treason of Stephen, entered Servia, ravaged it, led away as prisoners all the young men; the remainder of the inhabitants perished under the swords of the ferocious soldiers. To crown this act of barbarity, a magnificent banquet was served to the nobles of his court above the dead bodies of the Christians. Returning from Servia, he besieged Thessalonica, captured all the cities on the Strymon with exception of Zeitoun (Lamia); he then sent Ibrahim, son of Ali Pasha, to the Greek emperor to demand tribute.

Ibrahim, penetrated with horror for the tyranny of Musa, advised the foreign monarch to resist the demands, and instead of returning to the court of the sultan, he went to Brusa, bearing a letter from Manuel to Mahomet, who was then master of Asia Minor.

Incensed by the defection of Ibrahim, and still more irritated that the Emperor of Byzantium supported Ourkhan, son of Soliman, as his rival in Europe, and aided Mahomet to oppose him in Asia, Musa marched upon Constantinople, which saw itself besieged for the third time by the Ottomans. He burned all the neighboring villages, which were, however, deserted by the inhabitants, whom Manuel had received in his capital. The sultan was confident of obliging the city to open its gates; but his hopes were not realized, as his forces were unequal to the undertaking. Frequent sorties of the Greeks, skilfully directed, prevented him from approaching near the city. Still the besieged daily lost many of their brave defenders. The emperor was deeply afflicted. "I shall lose more," he said, "in losing ten soldiers out of a hundred, than if Musa were to lose a hundred out of a thousand."

Musa pushed the siege with unabated vigor, and the city was daily more closely pressed by his troops. The emperor, therefore, considered it more advantageous not to prolong the contention between the two Ottoman princes, but to send aid to Mahomet, the more formidable of the two sons of Bajazet, and engage him to cross into Europe and make common cause with him against Musa. Docile to the advice of Ibrahim Pasha, his vizier, Mahomet, whose progress had been arrested at Gallipoli, accepted the proposition of Manuel, and advanced with his army to Scutari. Being informed of his arrival on the Asiatic shore of the Bosphorus, the heir of the Cæsars went to meet the Mussulman prince on the imperial galley, concluded with him a treaty of peace and friendship, and conducted him to Constantinople. The noble stranger was welcomed with extraordinary magnificence, and his arrival was celebrated by festivities during three days. The fourth day Mahomet led his army, increased by the addition of a few Greeks, against Musa; but he was defeated and driven back into the city. A second attempt proved equally unsuccessful.

The Ottoman prince, afflicted by these two disasters, and tired of the inconstancy of fortune, whose changes he compared to the trembling of a leaf, said to the emperor: "Why do not you, who weigh affairs in a just scale, and who can foresee to which side it will incline, permit me in these evil days to leave you, so that either the enemy may be delivered into my hands, or that I may fall into his? I assure you that whatever has been decreed by God will infallibly happen. Allow me then to lead my forces to Adrianople; accompany me with your good wishes, and leave the rest to Providence." The emperor was touched by these words, and the following day the prince departed with his army, and crossed into Asia, where his presence was of importance in consequence of the successes of Djouneid, who had taken Smyrna and Ephesus. Djouneid, however, vainly attempted to hold out against Mahomet, and he was soon forced to submit.

Yacoub, governor of Angora, had likewise taken advantage of the absence of his sovereign to raise the standard of revolt. Compelled to sue for pardon, he obtained his life, but not his liberty.

These successes covered the arms of Mahomet with glory. The Prince of Soulkadr, his friend and ally, met him at the head of his forces in the plain of Angora, and they agreed to cross together into Europe, and endeavor, by a union with the Prince of Servia and the Emperor of Byzantium, to terminate these dissensions by a single blow. To carry this arrangement into effect, they went first to Constantinople, and thence Mahomet proceeded towards the north, in order to effect a junction with the Prince of Servia. He attacked Adrianople, which city refused to open its gates until he had conquered his brother's army. He therefore pursued the enemy towards Philippopolis, repulsed the troops of Musa at the famous defile of Succi, and entered the plain of Sofia, where he obtained an abundance of provisions. Encouraged by the protestations of fidelity of many nobles, he continued his march to the banks of the Morava without encountering the enemy. There he found Stephen, with the Servian army and several beys who had deserted the standard of Musa. The united armies pushed on to the banks of the Karrasson, and stopped two days in the plain of Tschamourli, where other officers of his brother came to present their homage.

The third day they perceived Musa slowly descending the mountain at the head of seven thousand Janizaries, whose services he had purchased at a high price. Mahomet drew up his forces in order of battle, and the two armies were confronting each other when Hasan, the aga of the Janizaries, who had deserted Musa and joined his brother, stepping in front of the ranks, addressed his former companions in arms in a loud voice: "Why do you delay to embrace the cause of the most virtuous and most just of the Ottoman princes? Why do you remain miserable and crushed by the tyranny of one who is not able to secure his own safety, much less to watch over others?"

This insolent speech excited the wrath of Musa, and followed by his Janizaries he precipitated himself upon Hasan, who immediately fled. Musa overtook him and with a stroke of his sabre cleft his head; but as he lifted his arm to deal another blow, a companion of the aga cut off the prince's hand. He was returning to his camp when the Janizaries, seeing the bloody arm of their sovereign, were seized with a panic terror and dispersed in every direction. Musa himself fled towards Walachia. Some knights who had been sent in pursuit, found him among the dead (1413). Thus finished the domination of Musa, a liberal prince, but so tyrannical in disposition that he alienated the affection of his beys and soldiers. His death terminated the war of succession which had desolated the Ottoman empire ever since the captivity of Bajazet. The conqueror ordered his brother's body to be conveyed to Brusa, and deposited in the tomb of their ancestors; he repaired to Adrianople to receive the oath of fidelity from the nobles of the state, who hastened to offer their homage.

The accession of Mahomet I. to the throne was

hailed with joy in the empire and the army. The new sultan was superior in every respect to his brothers. Whilst historians represent him to have been a remarkably handsome man, with the eye of an eagle and the strength of a lion, they also speak of him as a benevolent, generous, clement, and just prince, constant in his friendships, prudent and moderate. During his whole life, he was the faithful ally of the Byzantine emperor and the glorious support of the throne of Othman. To use the expression of a Turkish writer: "He was the Noah who saved from the deluge of the Tartars the ark of the empire beset by many dangers."

Upon learning the victory of Mahomet over the last and most powerful of his rivals, Manuel sent an embassy to congratulate him and to remind him of the promises he had made during his sojourn at Constantinople. Faithful to his word, the sultan respected the obligations imposed on him by gratitude, and restored to the emperor the castles which had been occupied on the Black Sea, the towns of Thessaly and the fortresses of the Propontis. He cemented the treaty by renewing his oath, made generous presents to the ambassadors, and dismissed them with words which testified his affection for their sovereign: "Say to the emperor, my father, that having been restored by the power of God and his assistance to the throne of my ancestors, I shall, in future, be as submissive to his will as a son should be to that of his father; that I shall preserve as long as I live the remembrance of his benefits, and that I shall seek every opportunity of doing him honor." No Mussulman prince had ever manifested a disposition so friendly towards the Greeks. Mahomet received at the same time the felicitations of the ambassadors of Servia, Walachia, Bulgaria, of the Duke of Janina, of the Despot of Lacedemon, and the Prince of Achaia. He invited all without distinction to his table, drank to their health, and said at parting with them: "Say to your masters that I offer them peace and I accept it from them. May God punish him who violates it!"

The emperor Manuel, delivered from all fear of his enemies, occupied himself with the marriage of his son John, to whom he destined the crown (1414). In order to strengthen the ties of friendship which united him with the Prince of Muscovia, he asked and obtained for his son the hand of Anne, the daughter of that prince. This marriage was not fortunate, for at the end of three years the young princess fell a victim to the plague, to the great regret of all the inhabitants.

The contagion swept off many others, among them one of the sons of Bajazet. Of the two who had been left by Soliman as hostages at Constantinople, the elder, Kasim, was sent away with his sister, Fatima. Joseph exhibited great talent for the Greek language and the sciences, and he had received instructions with John, the emperor's son. He frequently expressed a wish to be admitted to baptism, declaring that he was a Christian and did not believe in the doctrines of Mahomet. But the monarch opposed the administration of baptism to him, fearing to excite troubles on the part of the Turks, of whom a large number resided in Constantinople, and also of displeasing the sultan. When the scourge which was decimating the inhabitants of the capital struck him also, Joseph, feeling his death approaching, said to the emperor: "My lord and father, I am about to leave this world to appear before that tribunal which is prepared in the other. I profess myself a Christian, and you refuse me the seal of the faith, the pledge of the Holy Ghost. Know that if I die without baptism, I shall accuse you of it before God, the irreproachable and incorruptible Judge." Manuel, touched by these words, yielded to the desires of the prince, who received baptism with the sentiments of the liveliest faith, and died the following day. The funeral obsequies were celebrated with uncommon magnificence. The body was borne with great pomp to the Monastery of the Precursor and deposited in a marble tomb.

Three years afterwards, the eldest son of the emperor John married the daughter of the Marquis of Montferrat, a princess of great beauty, and according to the historians of the time, of fine character. The prince, nevertheless, conceived so great a dislike for her, that he left her always alone. Respect for his father's choice prevented him from sending her back to Italy, but when the young wife saw that his aversion continued to increase, she determined to leave Constantinople. She communicated her design to the Genoese of Galata, and one evening, attended by a numerous suite, she went to the garden as if for a walk. The Genoese received her on one of their galleys, and conveyed her to Pera, where she was received with all the honors due a sovereign. Her departure was known only in the morning of the following day, but no sooner was the news spread through the city, than the inhabitants in their indignation wished to destroy the quarter of the Genoese, to avenge what they called an insult. The emperor succeeded with difficulty in appeasing their anger; his son experienced the greatest satisfaction. The Genoese had in the port a merchant vessel about to set sail for Italy. The princess embarked as soon as the weather permitted, and arrived safely at Genoa. Her brother, accompanied by the whole court, met her on the confines of Montferrat, and escorted her to the palace of her ancestors. Shortly afterwards she retired into a monastery, and consecrated herself to God for the remainder of her life.

However, the heir of the throne, on whom Manuel had already bestowed the title of emperor, did not renounce marriage. He dispatched ambassadors to Alexis Coruncenes, Prince of Trebizond, to ask the hand of his daughter Mary, a princess as celebrated for her beauty as for the purity of her virtue and the gentleness of her disposition. The father having consented to the union, Mary left for Constantinople. She was welcomed amid the acclamations of the inhabitants, and having received the nuptial benediction from the patriarch Joseph, the young bride was proclaimed empress.

After the conclusion of the marriage festivities, the emperor undertook to chastise the Prince of Achaia, who had withdrawn from his obedience. He embarked with a few troops, made a descent upon Morea, recalled the rebel to his duty, and left his son Theodore at Lacedemon as despot. On his return he had an interview with Mahomet at Gallipoli. The sultan testified the greatest confidence in the sovereign, calling him his father.

Having no anxiety in regard to the Christians, Mahomet turned his arms against Asia Minor, where his presence was imperatively demanded by the revolt of Djouneid and the rupture of peace by the Prince of Caramania. The former, who had occupied in his own name Smyrna, Sardis and Philadelphia, was conquered; and Mahomet, yielding to the entreaties of the mother of the traitor, granted him pardon, requiring only an oath of fidelity to the Ottoman race. He defeated the Prince of Caramania and reduced him to submission.

Manuel, for his part, had taken advantage of the peace with the Ottomans to elevate on the isthmus of Corinth, for the distance of six miles, the wall which had been commenced by the ancient Greeks and repaired by Justinian, but which was now falling into ruins. He had seven sons; five had already received a portion of his States. John was associated with him in the government; Theodore was Despot of Lacedemon; Andronicus, of Thessalonica; Constantine, of Mesembria and Selymbria; André, of Riscinium in Dalmatia. At this period the islands of Negropont and Candia belonged to the Venetians; Chios and Lesbos, to the Genoese. The Acciainoli of Florence possessed a great part of Greece, which they had acquired in 1364 from Mary de Bourbon, Empress of Constantinople; their portion comprehended Achaia, Bœotia, Phocis and Athens. Etolia, Arcanania and Northern Epirus were governed by the family of Tocco. Southern

Epirus, or the principality of Albania, depended upon that of Pastriota, whose chief was then John Castriot.

Mahomet had succeeded in restoring peace to the provinces of the Ottoman empire, when an imposter, claiming to be the youngest son of Bajazet, who had disappeared at the battle of Ancyra, attempted to usurp the sovereign power. All the Ottoman historians designate him as the *false Mustapha*, but Byzantine writers maintain that he was really the son of Bajazet and the elder brother of Mahomet. However that may be, Mustapha proclaimed himself in Europe the true heir to the throne, and he was supported by Mirtsch, Prince of Wallachia, and by Djouneid, then governor of Nicopolis, the latter twice a rebel and twice restored to favor. The pretender crossed the Hermes, and marched towards Thessaly. Mahomet hastened to meet him, overtook him near Thessalonica, and was victorious in a pitched battle. Mustapha and Djouneid fled from the field, and sought refuge in the city, where they were kindly received by the governor, Demetrius Lascaris Leontarios, who promised them protection.

The following day, Mahomet sent to the Greek commander one of his officers, to claim the fugitives and to remind him of the friendship which united him with the emperors. "Spare your nation," he said, "spare your nation the woes which would overwhelm it were you to force me to turn my arms against her. The prey which has cast itself into your net is mine. It must be restored to me; otherwise I shall take your refusal as a signal for the rupture of peace, and I shall consider myself freed from any obligation in your regard. I will seize your city; all its inhabitants shall become my slaves; I will deprive you of life, and none of my enemies shall escape my vengeance." Leontarios, a man of consummate prudence, replied: "You know, my lord, that I am the servant of Mahomet as well as the servant of the emperor, whom you call your father. But if I am obliged to execute your orders, I must also notify the emperor, my master, of what has occurred. He who took refuge here, as a partridge pursued by a hawk, is a prince of the blood, your brother; but were he the lowest slave, I could not permit myself to violate rights so sacred without an order from the emperor. My master, I therefore humbly beg you to grant me time to write to him, and when I have received his orders, I will execute them with entire submission."

The sultan did not content himself with the answer of Leontarios. He transmitted directly to Manuel the demand he had made of the governor. "You know," replied the emperor to him, "that I promised to be a father to you, and you promised to be my son. If we both keep our promise, the fear of God will be before our eyes and we shall observe His commandments; if we fail in this, the father will be accused of having betrayed his son, and the son will be condemned as the murderer of the father. As for me, I keep my oath, and you violate yours. I will never deliver up to you fugitives who have claimed my protection; were I to do so, I should act as a tyrant, and not as a king. If my own brother were to cast himself into your arms as a place of refuge, you could not surrender him without violating the right of asylum. Know then that I will not commit so base an action. Nevertheless, as in our last treaty you acknowledge my paternal authority, I swear to you by the Holy Trinity, that during your reign and life, Mustapha and Djouneid shall not be set at liberty. After your death I shall act as circumstances may seem to require."

At the same time the following order was sent to Leontarios: "As soon as you receive these lines, place Mustapha and Djnoueïd on a galley and send them to Constantinople." Mahomet, fearing the dangerous consequences which might result from a rupture with the emperor, and being, moreover, satisfied that during his life the fugitives would not be at liberty, withdrew from Thessalonica and returned to Adrianople, freed from the anxiety caused by the revolt.

Demetrius executed the emperor's order, and Mahomet signed a treaty in virtue of which Manuel pledged himself to guard Mustapha, Djnoueïd and their thirty companions; and for this service the sultan was to pay annually the sum of three hundred thousand aspres. The negotiator of this treaty was Theologos Korax, a Greek of Philadelphia, a cunning, artful man, who, during the war between Tamerlane and Bajazet, had been administrator of his native city. He had there acquired an unenviable celebrity by delivering to the conquerors several of the principal citizens, whom the Tartar burned alive because they were unable to pay the contribution he had exacted of them. Later he found such favor with Mahomet and his vizier, Bajazet-Pasha, that he often had the honor of sitting at table with them, and by his influence he directed the most important negotiations. For this reason the emperor had appointed him his interpreter; he was, however, suspected of sacrificing the Greek interests to the Ottoman. Lest Korax should succeed in delivering Mustapha and Djnoueïd to Mahomet, they were sent to the island of Lemnos and kept under strict guard in the convent of the Blessed Virgin (1420).

Filled with resentment against Mirtsch, who had aided Mustapha in his attempted usurpation, Mahomet sent an army to ravage Wallachia. If the historian, Ducas, may be relied upon, he also cherished the design of being avenged on Constantinople; if so, he kept it secret. However, the very year that Manuel had pledged himself to retain Mustapha a prisoner, the sultan passed by Constantinople to go to Asia. The emperor was solicited by the archons to take advantage of the opportunity of securing Mahomet and his brother, but he refused to violate the sacred rights of hospitality. He sent Demetrius Leontarios, Isaac Hasan and Manuel Cantacuzenus, with many others, to meet him and offer him presents. The deputies received him outside the city and accompanied him to the shores of the Bosphorus. Manuel and his sons welcomed him on the imperial galley; another, magnificently decorated, was prepared for the sultan. The two sovereigns conversed amicably together, proceeding to Scutari, where Mahomet landed and entered the tent which had been arranged for him. The day passed in a friendly intercourse; towards evening, the sultan, mounting his horse, went to Nicomedia; the emperor returned by water to his capital.

In the following spring Mahomet returned to Adrianople by the way of Gallipoli, and Manuel again sent Leontarios to compliment him. The sultan received the deputy in the kindest manner. Three days afterwards, as he was engaged in hunting, he was struck with apoplexy and fell from his horse. His attendants bore him to his palace, where the most skilful physicians administered prompt remedies. Feeling that his end was near, he sent for his faithful vizier, Bajazet-Pasha, and conjured him in the name of God and the prophet to serve, with the same devotion of which he had given him so many proofs, his son, Amurat, the heir of the throne, who, being then governor of Amasia, was defending the eastern frontier of the empire against Kara-Juluk-Bianderi, a Turcoman lord of the dynasty of Mouton-Blanc. As to his two youngest sons, one of whom was seven and the other eight years of age, he confided them to the Greek emperor, hoping to secure for them a protector against the cruelty of their brother Amurat.

The day after the attack, Mahomet had sufficient strength to appear before the army, who welcomed him with their usual shouts of benediction and love. But the following day a second attack paralyzed his tongue, and he died in the evening (1421). Under these circumstances, the two viziers, Ibrahim and Bajazet, evinced much prudence and union. They kept secret the death of the sultan for forty days —until the arrival of his successor in the palace of Brusa.

Amurat II. attained the sovereign power at the age of eighteen. He prescribed a mourning of eight days for the obsequies of his father, whose remains were conveyed with great pomp to Bursa. He dispatched ambassadors to the court of the princes of Caramania and Mentesche, to King Sigismund and the emperor, to announce his accession to the throne and to renew the treaties signed by Mahomet. Peace was sworn with Caramania, and a truce of five years concluded with Hungary.

Before the arrival of the envoys at Constantinople, the Palæologus Lachynes and Theologos Korax had set out for Brusa, commissioned to demand the execution of Mahomet's testament, by which his two youngest sons had been confided to the care of the emperor. In case of refusal, they were to threaten Amurat with proclaiming Mustapha son and heir presumptive of Bajazet, master of Turkey in Europe. The vizier, Bajazet-Pasha, replied in the name of the sultan, "that it was not seemly, and moreover it was contrary to the laws of the prophet, to abandon the care and education of Mussulmans to infidels; that his master begged the emperor to renounce the guardianship, and to maintain the peace and friendship which the sultan was ready to confirm with oaths."

Manuel, upon receiving this reply, assembled his council; opinions were divided, but the prudence of the old Manuel yielded to the presumption of his son, John, and without considering the danger to which he was about to expose himself in the miserable condition of his empire, he sent Leontarios with ten well-armed galleys to the island of Lemnos, with orders to liberate Mustapha and Djnoueïd, and to convey them to the European continent. Leontarios made the pretender swear never to oppose the will of the emperor, to obey him as his father, and leave his son in his hands as a hostage and a pledge of his fidelity to his oath. Mustapha submitted to every condition required of him. He promised, if success crowned his arms, to restore Gallipoli to Manuel, as also all the coast north of Constantinople as far as Wallachia, and on the south the cities of Thessaly as far as Erysos and Mount Athos.

After the conclusion of the treaty confirmed by oath, Leontarios landed under the walls of Gallipoli with Mustapha and Djnoueïd. Many of the inhabitants of the city and neighboring country ranged themselves under the standard of the pretended son of Bajazet, and acknowledged him as the legitimate heir of the throne; but the garrison remained faithful to Amurat, and refused to surrender the castle. Leaving Demetrius to continue the siege of Gallipoli, Mustapha marched with his partisans, whose numbers increased hourly, towards the promontory of Athos called Hexamilon, and he soon obtained possession of several places which, considering him the legitimate heir, opened their gates without opposition.

This news reached Bursa whilst the new sultan was still receiving the submission of the people, who hastened in crowds to testify to him their sorrow for the death of his father and their joy at his accession to the throne. The nobles of the court, particularly the viziers Ibrahim-Pasha and Aüvaz-Pasha, who detested the insupportable pride of Bajazet-Pasha, and viewed with a jealous eye his wealth and influence, persuaded Amurat to send him to Europe to appease the storm. Bajazet embarked with a small number of soldiers, and sailed through the middle of the Bosphorus, in order to avoid the Greek galleys. He then marched towards Adrianople, collected all the forces of Roumilia, thus increasing his army to thirty thousand men, and encamped in a marshy plain, whence the city could be only imperfectly seen, on account of the woods which covered it. Mustapha, having been joined by some of the great vassals of the empire, advanced to meet the enemy.

The two armies were facing each other, when Mustapha addressed the troops of Amurat, crying out to them that they ought not to refuse obedience to the real heir of the throne of Othman. Immediately, as if struck by a magic power, the army of Amurat deserted to the standard of Mustapha. Bajazet, seeing himself thus abandoned, considered by what means he could escape destruction; he alighted from his horse, and with his brother, Hamsa, prostrated himself at the feet of the victor. Thus delivered from the uncertain event of a battle, Mustapha was proclaimed by the troops the sovereign lord of Roumania. Bajazet and Hamsa were brought before him in chains. Mustapha delivered them into the hands of Djnoueïd as his captives; by his orders the vizier was beheaded, but he restored Hamsa to liberty, little suspecting how dearly he was hereafter to pay for that act of clemency. This easy triumph augmented Mustapha's confidence; he advanced with his army to Adrianople. The inhabitants met him outside the city, and testified by their acclamations their joy at his success.

The garrison of Gallipoli, considering it useless to prolong their resistance, surrendered to Leontarios. According to the conditions of the treaty recently signed, the servant of Manuel expected to take possession in the name of his master. He had already made arrangements to convey arms and ammunition into the fortress, when Djnoueïd appeared, and dissipated his dreams of conquest. "It was not," he said, "for the Greek emperor that we fought and incurred so many dangers. To God alone we owe the victory, and to God alone we return thanks. But as you shared the labors and fatigues by which we obtained success, we will recompense you by suitable presents, and by a continuation of our friendship. But do not imagine that we shall bestow upon you fortresses and cities. Be grateful that we allow you to return to Constantinople; we have not forgotten the ill treatment we received at Lemnos. I say to you, as the wolf in the proverb: your head is your recompense. Set sail at once for Constantinople: the wind is favorable. Salute the emperor in our name; tell him in what manner God gave us the victory; let him preserve his friendship for us, and we assure him in return of ours; but let him not claim Gallipoli."

Indignant as well as surprised by this discourse, Leontarios replied briefly to the audacious Djnoueïd, extolling the wisdom and courage of the emperor, and at the same time uttering menaces. He withdrew to his galleys, uncertain what course to pursue. Mustapha arrived soon after, and said likewise: "I did not take up arms for the advantage of the Emperor Manuel; I remember the oath I made to the prophet to reconquer the cities of Islamism; among them is Gallipoli. I prefer at the terrible day of judgment to render an account of my oath to the emperor, to answering for the surrender of a Mussulman city into the hands of the infidels. I will observe the other conditions of the treaty which bind me to your master; you are free to return to Constantinople."

Thus was Greek policy foiled in the advantages it hoped to derive from the liberty and support granted to the pretender. Leontarios set sail for Constantinople. The perfidious conduct of Mustapha filled Manuel with anger and grief. After long wavering as to the course to be pursued, he decided to renew with Amurat the existing treaties, but to demand of him at the same time the guardianship of the sultan's two younger brothers. His intentions were anticipated by a message from Amurat, who sent the grand vizier, Ibrahim Pasha, to offer him on the part of his master peace and friendship. He endeavored to persuade the emperor to furnish aid to the son of Mahomet, his old and faithful ally against Mustapha. Manuel still insisted that the young princes should be confided to his care, but as Ibrahim was unwilling to accede to the proposition, negotiations were broken off. In the meantime, Amurat had been strengthened by an alliance with an Italian people.

A Genoese colony established at Phocæa, on the coast of Ionia, was enriching itself by the monopoly of alum, and by the payment of an annual tribute it secured for its flag many privileges from the Ottomans. The governor of the Genoese, the ambitious

John Adorno, son of the doge, being informed of the enterprise of Mustapha, embraced the cause of Amurat, and made him an offer of vessels. The sultan, learning that the pretender was wasting his time in dissipation, and that he had irritated Manuel by the refusal to surrender Gallipoli, did not reject a proposition which would help to restore to him the inheritance of his father. He replied to the Genoese by assurances of friendship, and sent an intelligent and able Turk with fifty thousand ducats to fit out the vessels necessasy to transport his army into Europe.

In the meanwhile Mustapha, proud of his victory, abandoned himself to every excess. His favorite, Djnoueïd, aroused him from his unworthy inactivity by imparting to him news of the danger which menaced him from the preparations of Amurat. He advised him to combat the ally of the Genoese in Asia, and not allow him to embark from Lampsacus or Scutari. Djnoueïd was not actuated in his advice by devotion to the interests of Mustapha, but by the thought of a new treachery which he was contemplating, and by means of which he hoped to escape the consequences of an undertaking which he regarded as desperate. The pretender followed the counsels of Djnoueïd, and landed with his army at Lampsacus, where he remained three days. Amurat immediately left Brusa and took up a position beyond the river Ryndacus. There, surrounded by faithful servants, he watched every movement of the enemy, who before long approached the opposite bank. The two armies were about to engage, when a large portion of the troops of Mustapha passed over to the standard of his rival. His numbers were still sufficient to leave him a hope of victory, but the defection of Djnoueïd spread a panic terror throughout the camp, and his army dispersed in every direction; he himself galloped at full speed towards Lampsacus. Fortunately he found a bark in which he reached Gallipoli, with no other escort than his household servants.

Master of the field without having struck a blow, Amurat directed his steps towards Lampsacus (Lampsaki), and met between this city and Gallipoli the podesta Adorno, who, faithful to his promises, was awaiting his arrival with a squadron of seven vessels of war. The sultan, accompanied by five hundred guards, entered the largest, the crew of which was composed of eight hundred of their bravest men; he entrusted to them his liberty and his life. The other vessels carried, each, an equal number of Turks and Franks.

When, from the height of the ramparts of Gallipoli, Mustapha saw the enormous vessels covering the water like so many islands, he was agitated by the darkest presentiments. He sent to demand from Adorno an interview with one of his officers. He offered him fifty thousand ducats if he would betray Amurat into his hands. Adorno indignantly rejected the proposition. The troops disembarked in sight of Mustapha, whose soldiers protected the port. Not being disposed to defend the falling fortunes of their master, they fled as soon as the archers poured on them a shower of arrows. The pretender, betrayed a second time, fled to Adrianople, collected together his treasures, and continued his flight towards Wallachia.

Amurat, thus favored by the chances of war, delayed three days at Gallipoli, put to death the soldiers who had opposed his debarkation, and marched to the conquest of Adrianople with Adorno, his marines, and two thousand Italians armed with lances and battle-axes. The inhabitants of Adrianople met him in crowds. He received them with extreme kindness, and invited them all to a splendid banquet spread out in his father's palace. Adorno, his officers, and even his soldiers, were likewise entertained, and on this occasion the sultan recompensed the services of the podesta by bestowing upon him the castle of Perithoreon, and during his life the revenues of the new Phocœa. The captains and sailors of the Genoese fleet were also generously rewarded. Mustapha was pursued and captured by his own servants, and delivered to Amurat. The sultan ordered him to be hung on the public road as a common criminal, in order to confirm by the ignominy of his death the general impression of the Ottomans that he was an imposter artfully brought forward by the Emperor Manuel.

Being now rid of the rival who had been opposed to him by the perfidious counsels of the emperor, the sultan resumed against Constantinople the projects of vengeance which prudence had forced him to defer, but which were to be not the less terrible from the delay. Thus recommenced the war of Islamism against Christianity, a war destined to be the last for the empire, and which was to plant the Crescent upon its ruins, and bear it triumphant to the shores of the Danube.

CHAPTER V.

PROGRESS OF THE OTTOMANS—UNION OF THE CHURCHES.

Embassy of Manuel to the Sultan—March of the Ottomans upon Constantinople—Theologos Korax accused of betraying the Greeks—His death—Siege of Constantinople by Amurat—Defence of the Greeks—Revolt and death of Mustapha, brother of Amurat—Success of the Ottoman generals in Europe—Death of the Emperor Manuel—John II. Palæologus his successor—Treaty of John Palæologus with Amurat—Insolence of Djnoueïd punished—Amurat refuses to treat with the Venetians—Siege and capture of Thessalonica by the Turks—Surrender of Janina—Hostilities against Servia, Wallachia, and Hungary—Negotiations of John Palæologus with the Latins for the union of the two Churches—Council of the Greeks and Latins at Ferrara and Florence—Union of the two Churches—General discontent—Metrophanes elevated to the See of Constantinople.

WHEN Manuel saw the whole edifice of his policy crumble beneath his feet, he sent as ambassadors to the victor two men of noble birth and highly esteemed for their prudence and wisdom, Palæologus Lachanes and Marcus Jagaries. They were deputed to felicitate the sultan upon the death of the usurper, and to try to convince him that their master was not to blame in what had happened; that the Vizier Bajazet was answerable for the rupture of the negotiations; in a word, they were to make every effort to disarm his anger. But Amurat had forgotten none of his causes of complaint against the emperor; he refused to admit the ambassadors until he had completed his arrangements. When his army was prepared to march upon Constantinople, he dismissed them, saying: "Assure the emperor that I

(126)

shall soon visit him." After a few days he set out at the head of twenty thousand men to besiege the capital of the Byzantine empire (1422).

The approach of the troops of Amurat dismayed the people. They dreaded the struggle with a warlike and barbarous nation animated by fanaticism, the conquerors of so many Burgundian and French cavaliers at Nicopolis, whose former successes contributed to augment their desire for conquest. Manuel's subjects remarked with dismay that whilst the Turks were real barbarians in their customs, they had borrowed from Greek civilization all those arts of warfare which might assure them victory, such as machines of war, a certain kind of tactics, and the sort of discipline which had made the Byzantine troops effective. Their sultans had rendered them more formidable by restraining their impetuosity and by creating among them the Spahis and Janissaries, disciplined and permanent bodies of soldiers.

The inhabitants in the midst of these alarms imagined that Theologos Korax had provoked hostilities by his acts, because he had not been sent on the late embassy to the sultan; and they indulged in bitter invectives against him. The emperor, to lull these suspicions and calm the excitement, deputed this man to go to Amurat, who had already placed his camp before the walls of the city. Korax held a long conference with the sultan, without any result. One of his most intimate friends asserted that he had heard him promise to deliver the city upon condition that Amurat would confide the government of it to him. As the accused left the monastery where

Manuel was remaining, Prince John, who was engaged in superintending the defence of the ramparts, was suddenly overwhelmed with insults by the inhabitants and soldiery. The old emperor, hearing the tumult, demanded the cause. They led into his presence the man who had discovered the perfidy. Manuel ordered him to be guarded with Korax, that the truth of the accusation might be investigated the following day.

Dissatisfied with the indulgence of the sovereign, and incensed to find the interests of Constantinople betrayed by those who derived thence their fortune and glory, the guard of the corps of Cretans revolted, and demanded that the interpreter should be delivered to them. Manuel dared not resist the furious multitude that beset his palace, and he allowed them to take the unhappy ambassador from prison, to acquit him if innocent, or condemn him if guilty. The soldiers hastened to his house, where they found writings against the emperor, precious stuffs, vessels of gold and silver which had been entrusted to him by the sultan for his master, and which they accused him of retaining for himself. The soldiers dragged him from the prison to the imperial palace, plucked out his eyes, tore the flesh from his face, and cast him thus mutilated into a dungeon, where he expired after three days of frightful torture. His house was plundered, and then burned to the ground.

Amurat learned with regret and anger the cause and manner of the death of Korax, to whom he had always testified much kindness. He attributed this tragic end to the calumnies of another Greek interpreter, the Ephesian Michael Pyllis, a man of noble birth, and a Christian, employed as a secretary in the imperial palace. This man had become an object of general aversion. Unfortunately for himself, he was at that time in the camp of the sultan; the Turks seized and tortured him. The following day they kindled an immense fire, and threatened to cast him alive into the flames unless he renounced his faith. The wretch consented to profess Islamism publicly, and he terminated his life long afterwards in his apostasy.

Early in June, Michael Bey appeared under the walls of Constantinople with an army ten thousand strong, devastated the surrounding country, burned the villages, destroyed the grain, killed the cattle, and reduced the inhabitants to slavery. Ten days later the besieging army arrived, and finding only ruins, vented their rage by uprooting the olive-trees and vines. Lastly came Amurat himself, proud of his recent victory and inflamed with anger against the Christians. In imagination he had completed the conquest of the city, and inundated the country, changed into a desert, with his infidel hordes. He ordered immediately the construction of a wall which was to extend from the Golden Gate to the Gate of Bois. This rampart, only an arrow-shot distant from the city, formed of enormous posts, filled in the intervals with fascines and earth, and supported by hurdles, could resist the stones thrown from machines and the discharge of fire-arms. Directing their principal attack against an old tower, the besiegers drew to the walls, on wheels, wooden towers of the same height as those within the city. The soldiers, animated by the presence of the sultan, displayed a wonderful activity; a portion fabricated machines to be used in the assault, others dug mines by which to secure a subterranean entrance within the walls.

In order to excite the courage of the troops and augment the number of the besiegers, Amurat proclaimed that *Constantinople and all its treasures should be abandoned to the Mussulmans.* The prospect of conquering the city of the Cæsars and the hope of booty attracted from Asia pious volunteers, who aspired to the crown of martyrdom, and a multitude of those who had no regular occupation. The Ottoman camp was soon filled with cattle and slave dealers, usurers, and others of the same stamp, calculating already the value of the booty which they expected to fall to the victors. Many dervishes, also coveting a portion of the prey, hastened to the army. Among these one was particularly noticed for his handsome countenance and imposing appearance—the grand Scheick Seid-Bochari, emir-sultan—son-in-law of Bajazet Ilderim. Proud of his descent from the prophet, of his alliance with the family of the sultan, and of the accomplishment of his prediction as to the event of the battle of Ouloubad (Ryndacus), he advanced, mounted on a mule and surrounded by a crowd of fanatic dervishes who strove to kiss his hands, his feet, and even the trappings of his mule.

As soon as Seid-Bochari, whose presence was to consecrate Amurat's enterprise, had alighted, he retired to his tent to consult the books of the soothsayers, in order to fix the day and hour when the ramparts of the city would fall under the Moslem assault. Whilst he was thus engaged in consulting the prophet, the dervishes, his companions, filled the air with frightful shrieks and insulted the defenders of Constantinople. "Where is your God, blind Greeks?" they exclaimed; "where is your Christ? Where the saints who should protect you? To-morrow we shall enter your city; to-morrow we shall lead you into slavery with your wives and children. The prophet has so decreed."

At last the emir-sultan emerged from his tent, and announced in a solemn voice, as though inspired by God, that on Monday, August 24, 1422, at one o'clock in the afternoon, he would mount his charger, would wave his drawn sword, thrice utter the war-cry, and that the city would immediately fall into the hands of the Ottomans. On the appointed day and hour, Bochari mounted a superb courser; he approached the ramparts with the majesty of a prophet, escorted by five hundred dervishes and preceded by an immense shield. The pious procession thrice uttered the Turkish war-cry. The emir-sultan drew his cimeter, cried in a loud voice "*Allah! Mahomet!*" pushed his charger to a gallop, and ordered a general assault. Immediately the combat commenced throughout the whole length of the wall on the side of the land from the Golden Gate to the Gate of Bois. The Emperor Manuel was dying. John, the heir of the throne, took his stand outside the Gate Saint Romain, encouraging the soldiers and the inhabitants to defend courageously their faith, their homes and their liberty against the Mussulmans. The whole population was under arms; women and children used scythes for sabres, and the heads of casks for shields; the arrows fell so thick and fast that the light of the sun was obscured. The archons and the ephors at the head of the besieged combated the viziers and the emirs of the Turks. The Greek monks and priests wished likewise to share the danger with their fellow-citizens, and fought valiantly by their side. In the midst of the hissing of the flying arrows and the clashing of arms, in the height of the combat, *Allah* and *Mahomet* resounded from the ranks of the Mussulmans; *Christ* and *Panagia* (Blessed Virgin) was echoed back by the Greeks. Never was there a more hotly contested battle, never was there a more frightful tumult. The sun was sinking below the horizon, and still the Greeks continued to repel with heroic courage the attacks of their numerous enemies, when the Turks desisted from the combat, set fire to their machines, and fled as if miraculously repulsed, thus giving the lie to their fanatical imposter.

The inhabitants attributed the miracle to the *Panagia*. The historian Canano relates that the emir-sultan asserted that a beautiful virgin, clothed in blue, and surrounded by a dazzling light, had traversed the rampart when the assault was the most furious, and at the sight of this supernatural apparition, the besiegers were panic stricken, and fled in disorder to their camp. An extraordinary circumstance attending this attack was the small loss experienced on both sides. After this terrible struggle, the Turks left only one thousand dead on the field; the Greeks had only thirty killed and seventy wounded. They pursued the enemy, and obtained possession of several machines and cannons. The employment of the latter destructive invention was advised by the Genoese, who were ever ready to sacrifice every other sentiment to their mercantile cupidity.

Turkish authors explain the retreat of the Ottomans in the following manner: Although his prostration was so extreme as to convince him that death was near at hand, the Emperor Manuel had recourse to every expedient which his Greek policy could suggest to rid himself of his formidable enemy. At the very moment that the sultan was advancing against Byzantium, he succeeded in bringing forward a new rival in the person of another Mustapha, brother of the sultan, only fifteen years of age. He had taken refuge with his tutor, Elias, in Caramania, whence the emperor recalled him to Asia Minor, Whilst he was conducting the siege of Constantinople, Amurat learned that his brother had raised the standard of revolt, for the purpose of disputing the crown with him, and that he had obtained possession of Nicæa. This unexpected news forced him to abandon at once the siege of the capital of the Byzantine empire, and return to Asia, where his presence alone could quell the insurrection. Before his departure he appointed the son of Eurenos governor of Roumilia, and confided to Firouz Bey the command of the troops destined to operate in the north against Wallachia.

Amurat was marching against Mustapha, when the young prince secretly left his camp and visited Manuel at Constantinople. He remained with him several days in order to secure the assistance of the Greeks, and returned to Asia by the way of Selymbria. But in the meantime Elias had been bought over to betray his master to the sultan by the promise of the government of Anatolia. The traitor seized the prince, conducted him to the camp of Amurat, and placed him in the hands of Mezid-Bey. By the sultan's order, Mustapha was hung on a fig-tree before the gates of Nicæa. His body was taken to Brusa and laid in the tomb beside his father, Mahomet I.

Although the death of this second competitor for the throne had put an end to domestic dissensions, Amurat remained in Asia for the purpose of reducing to submission the prince of Sinope, who wished to render himself independent of the sultan. In Europe success had crowned the arms of his generals; in the north Firouz-Bey had forced Urakul, prince of Wallachia, to purchase peace by the payment of the tribute which had been due for two years; in the south the son of Eurenos had continued hostilities against the Greeks. He penetrated into Peloponnesus, took Lacedemon, Gardica and Tavia, and gained near the latter city a signal victory over the Albanian forces. In imitation of Tamerlane, he erected a pyramid with the skulls of eight hundred prisoners.

After having conquered the prince of Sinope, and granted him peace upon condition of obtaining the hand of his daughter in marriage, with the rich mines of Kastemouni as her dower, the sultan returned to Adrianople. Here he received his betrothed with all the honors due her exalted rank, and celebrated his marriage with great magnificence. Whilst the son of Mahomet was leading his Janissaries to victory, both in Europe and Asia, the old Manuel terminated his miserable life. Towards the end of his days he had associated with him his son, John II. Palæologus, and had almost entirely left to him the care of government. He died clothed in the monastic habit (1425). His son, John II., succeeded him, being recognized as sole emperor of the Greeks.

The same year Amurat consoled himself for the failure of his attack upon Constantinople by an expedition into central Greece. The Prince of Albania submitted to him, and as a pledge of his fidelity, delivered to him his four sons, who thenceforth remained in the service of the Sublime Porte. The youngest, Georges, was remarkable for the beauty of his features, his personal graces and his talents. Returning to Adrianople, the sultan made a treaty with John II., to whom he gave the permission to reign in consideration of an annual tribute of three hundred thousand aspres, or thirty thousand ducats, and the cession of the cities and fortresses situated on the Black Sea, with the exception of Selymbria and Deikos, the two advance posts of the capital, and the other places on the Strymon. John Palæologus flattered himself with having thus purchased a tranquillity which would be undisturbed by either foreign or domestic foes. His brother Constantine had exchanged his cities of Mesembria and Selymbria for the principality of Lacedemon, and he thus formed in Peloponnesus a domination respected by the neighboring powers. His brother

Andronicus had ceded his city of Thessalonica to the Venetians, upon the promise that the inhabitants should be protected and enjoy the rights of citizens of Venice; he hoped from their maritime prosperity to be able to make an advantageous alliance with them against the Ottomans.

About this period Amurat renewed the treaty of peace formerly existing with the princes of Servia and Wallachia, and signed a truce of two years with Sigismund, King of Hungary, who had been recently elected Emperor of Germany. The two sovereigns exchanged rich presents, the sultan sending gold and silk fabrics, vases and ornamental carpets, and Sigismund returning gold pommels, pieces of velvet and cloth, six race-horses, and a thousand gold florins.

Being at peace with foreign princes, Amurat took advantage of the temporary tranquillity to punish Djnoueïd, who after his restoration to the government of Aïdin, had refused to acknowledge the suzerainty of the Sublime Porte. Brave and skilful, but unquiet and turbulent, Djnoueïd had lent his aid to every revolt as it arose; he was at last overpowered by Khalil, whom the sultan deputed to subdue the rebel. Djnoueïd, seeing the impossibility of resistance to forces so far superior to his own, surrendered to Amurat's lieutenant, who promised him a safe conduct. But Hamsa Bey, a relation of Khalil and brother of Bajazet Pasha, whom Djnoueïd had put to death, sent four executioners in the night, charged to strangle the prisoner and his family. Their heads were sent to Adrianople and placed at the sultan's feet.

Being thus delivered from his dangerous enemy, the Ottoman sovereign repaired to Ephesus, to receive the ambassadors of the princes of Europe and Asia, his vassals, who came on the part of their masters to offer their congratulations. Among them appeared the envoys of Dan of Wallachia, of Layar, despot of Servia, and Lucas Notaras, prime minister of the Emperor of Byzantium; also Genoese from Chios, and even Knights of St. John of Jerusalem from the island of Rhodes. He renewed his alliance with all excepting the Venetians. "The city of Thessalonica," said Amurat, "forms a part of my inheritance; Bajazet, my grandfather, took it from the Romans by force of arms; if the Romans had reconquered it they would refuse to restore it to me, and would accuse me of injustice if I asked it of them; but by what right do you, who are Latins from Italy, claim it? Unless you withdraw promptly, I shall expel you by force."

Anxious to preserve peace, the Venetians endeavored, without success, to make a treaty which would insure their tranquillity. Amurat ordered preparations to be made for an expedition against Thessalonica. As soon as they were completed he went to Seues, recalled his lieutenant, Hamsa-Bey, from Asia, and sent him to invest that important city. Hamsa soon appeared under the ramparts, at the head of an army a hundred times more numerous than that of the besieged (1429).

The Venetians, determined to defend the city to the last extremity, placed the garrison at different points of the walls; but their numbers were so small that two or even three bastions were in some parts manned by only one or two soldiers. On the 26th of February a violent earthquake shook the ground, and in the midst of the general terror, some Turkish soldiers penetrated into the city, hoping to come to an agreement with the inhabitants, by which they might take possession in the name of Amurat without making an attack. Many of the Greeks favored the proposition, and the attempt might have proved successful, but for the distrust of the Venetians, which was pushed so far, that in relieving the sentinels they always placed by the side of every Greek soldier a man taken from the mercenary troops, which were made up of all nationalities. In vain Hamsa thrice summoned the besieged to surrender, promising to spare the city and grant their liberty to the citizens; in vain he shot arrows wrapped in letters confirming these assurances with oaths. The Venetians would listen to no proposition which involved their submission; and the Greeks, who entered into the views of the enemy, were held in check by force.

Under these circumstances, Hamsa, having prepared a large number of scaling ladders and other suitable machines of war, sent messengers to Amurat, begging him to give the order for the assault before the arrival of the troops which the besieged were expecting from Venice. The sultan came in person, and determined upon the sack of Thessalonica. But the place was strong, and his troops were opposed by men of determination. The night of the 1st of March a report was circulated that a general assault was to be made the following day. The people filled the churches. imploring the protection of

Heaven against the barbarous Ottomans. The Venetians withdrew from the ramparts a portion of the garrison, at most consisting of fifteen hundred men, to protect the port, fearing that the Turks would seek to burn those galleys of the republic which had arrived during the day. The Greeks, not understanding the cause of this movement, supposed that the Venetians had renounced the idea of defending the city, and they returned to their homes.

At the break of day, the Turks, inflamed with a thirst for blood and pillage, rushed to the assault. Amurat sounded the trumpet, and proclaimed that all the booty should be abandoned to the soldiers, that he reserved for himself only the city. The army surrounded Thessalonica from east to west; on the eastern side, where the walls were the weakest, was placed a chosen corps under the orders of the sultan himself, who, by his presence, animated the assailants to extraordinary exertion, and urged them on by presents and promises of future rewards. He distributed garments of silk to the bravest, and paid for every stone removed from a bastion the same price as for a prisoner. The arrows shot by the Turks fell so thick and fast that the Venetians were scarcely able to remain long enough upon the parapets to hurl blindly a few heavy stones upon the assailants, to prevent them from mounting the ladders. Still, they succeeded in precipitating many into the trenches. At last, a soldier, holding his sabre between his teeth, gained the summit of the tower of the Trigonon, killed the sentinel, and threw his head over the wall. The Greeks, supposing that the ramparts had been carried, dispersed in every direction. The example of their intrepid companion excited the Turks to redouble their efforts; they placed scaling ladders against the Trigonon and the Tower of Samaro, and the bastion was taken amid the clashing of timbrels.

Resistance was now impossible, and the besieged thought only of means of escape; they concealed themselves in every available place, or endeavored to reach the port, hoping to be able to make a stand there, as it was well fortified. Upon reaching the outer wall, they found the Venetians collected in a body; but, overcome by terror, they soon cast themselves into the sea and made for the galleys, which were anchored near. The Ottoman army, scaling walls or opening a way through the mines, penetrated Thessalonica on all sides, and rushed in a body towards the harbor, where the inhabitants had sought refuge after the departure of the Venetians. Then commenced the usual scenes of horror, the general pillage and the pursuit of slaves. The ferocious hordes of Amurat were touched neither by the tears of innocence, the groans of old age, nor the cries of infancy; under all circumstances they were without pity. Women were torn from the arms of their husbands; children from their mothers' breast. All who made the least resistance were massacred. It was estimated that seven thousand were reduced to slavery. Not a house, not a palace escaped devastation; not a church profanation. Among the prisoners, a few women gained over by deceitful promises, and men yielding to the violence of torture, informed the enemy that the most valuable articles and the treasures had been concealed in the churches under the altars; the Turks overthrew them and left not a stone upon a stone. The ornaments and pictures were committed to the flames or broken to pieces. The tomb of St. Demetrius was opened, and the body cut in bits, which were scattered in every direction. Such was the immense destruction which attended the capture of Thessalonica. The historian, Ducas, however, says that this is but a feeble image, a slight disaster, compared with the violence and cruelty which was soon to afflict the capital of the empire.

When the troops were satiated with the work of plunder, Amurat took possession of the city, and permitted the prisoners who had fallen to his share to return to their dwellings. He supplied the places of those who had been killed or made slaves by families brought in from neighboring villages. The sultan converted into mosques the church of Saint Mary and the convent of St. John the Precursor. He did not, however, profane the church of St. Demetrius; on the contrary, he visited it and restored it to the Christians. The Turks contented themselves with removing from other religious edifices an immense quantity of slabs of marble, intending to convey them to Adrianople. The Greeks, who had hoped to find in Amurat the benefactor as well as the conqueror of Thessalonica, soon saw the hopes they had cherished fade away. The sultan claimed the most beautiful edifices as his private property, bestowed the finest palaces upon his principal officers, and transformed all the temples but four into mosques. The cloisters became caravansaries, and the stones of the demolished churches were used for the construction of a Turkish bath in the centre of the city. "Thessalonica," says Joannes Anagnosa, an eye-witness of her disaster, "Thessalonica, humbled and defiled, shed bitter tears; she mourned because she had not been annihilated by an earthquake, swallowed up by the waves of the sea, or devoured by the flames. Better would it have been," he exclaimed in his affliction, "that she had never existed, than to have been thus outraged and destroyed."

Thus Thessalonica, conquered in 1386 by Amurat I., restored to the Byzantines, retaken eight years afterwards by Bajazet, and later by Mahomet, fell at last for the fourth time into the power of the Ottomans, and thenceforth, it belonged to their empire under the name of Salonica. Notwithstanding the many times it had been pillaged, the city, built an amphitheatre at the foot of Mount Kurtiath, with a harbor capable of containing three hundred vessels, recuperated rapidly, as its advantageous position rendered it necessarily the commercial mart of Thrace and Thessaly. At the present time it contains about eighty thousand inhabitants.

The loss of Thessalonica was a bitter sorrow to the Venetians. Fearing to be deprived also of the island of Negropont, they sent ambassadors to the sultan shortly after his return to Adrianople, and concluded with him a treaty of peace.

In this same year (1413) died John Castiota, lord of Southern Albania. Amurat, who held the four sons of this prince as hostages, took possession of Croïa and the surrounding country. Peloponnesus owed its safety only to a new movement on the part of the emir of Caramania, who lost no opportunity of regaining the power which had been lost by his ancestors. The theft of a beautiful Arabian charger, which the prince had taken from the chief of the Turcomans of Soulkadr, was the frivolous pretext for the war. The chief complained to the sultan, who punished the prince by depriving him of two cities, and he made peace only at the entreaties of his sister, the wife of the emir.

A Wallachian lord, named Wlad-Drakal, (in their language the *Devil*), a cunning and bad man, well deserving the name he bore, had assassinated his sovereign, who had just concluded a treaty of peace with the sultan. Amurat determined at first to support the claim of the legitimate heir, brother of the deceased prince; but a promise made by the usurper to pay tribute, and acknowledge himself the vassal of the Porte, soon removed his scruples. The following year (1433) he considered it advantageous to preserve friendly relations with the King of Hungary, and to congratulate him upon his accession to the throne of Germany. Sigismund received the ambassadors in the cathedral of Basle. The envoys presented him, in the name of their master, with twelve golden goblets filled with gold coin, and mantles of silk embroidered with gold and precious stones.

Bulgaria had ceased to exist as an independent principality after the death of its last prince, during the reign of Bajazet; the chiefs of Servia were tributaries of the Turks, and often their efficient allies. The despot, Stephen V., who had saved Soliman at the battle of Angora, recommended on his deathbed the aged George Brankovich as his successor. Summoned by Amurat to surrender Servia, George purchased peace by promising the sultan his daughter Mara in marriage, and a portion of his States for her dower. In return, he obtained permission to erect a citadel at Semendra, on the banks of the Danube, in order to protect himself against Hungary. The sultan celebrated his marriage with great magnificence.

Early in the spring Amurat conceived a detestable design against his father-in-law, being urged to it by a certain Fadulac, an uncompromising enemy of the Christians. This Fadulac had formerly collected the revenues of the Turkish empire. His great business capacity, and his hatred against the adorers of Christ, had elevated him to the dignity of vizier. In conversation one day with the sultan he said to him: "Why, my lord, do you not exterminate the enemies of our faith? Instead of using the power placed in your hands by God according to his will, you favor the infidels. This is not what God expects of you; he wishes your sword to destroy these wretches, until they become converted and embrace the doctrine of God and the prophet. Reflect, my lord, that contrary to our interests you have permitted the prince of Servia to erect a fort. If you expel him from it, we shall have an unobstructed road to Hungary. We shall thence obtain an abundance of gold, and having become masters of that country, we shall be able to crush the enemies of our faith in Italy."

The sultan listened willingly to the suggestions of his vizier, and as the first step towards the completion of his designs, he demanded of his father-in-law the cession of the fortress of Semendra. Being advised to undertake hostilities against Drakal of Wallachia, he summoned him, as well as George, to present themselves at his court. Instead of obeying the order, George fortified Semendra more strongly, and appealed to Sigismund for aid. The King of Hungary, notwithstanding the apparent friendship existing between himself and Amurat, had kept up a secret intercourse with his enemies, and considered the present a favorable time for renewing the struggle with the Turks. George yielded to him his fortified town of Belgrade in exchange for some cities in Hungary. Sigismund bore the brunt of the sultan's anger. During forty-five days the Ottoman army devastated the country, and carried away on its departure seventy thousand prisoners. The death of the King of Hungary saved the Turks from the effects of his vengeance. His three crowns of Hungary, Bohemia, and Germany did not descend peacefully to his son-in-law, Albert, and his daughter Elizabeth. In a few days a bloody contest arose between the Hungarians of Buda and the Germans of Albert's followers. The murder of a Hungarian noble was avenged by the massacre of all foreigners, Germans, Bohemians, and Italians; but Albert found it necessary to pardon the crime, in order to preserve his crown.

Emboldened by the death of Sigismund, the Turks invaded Servia. At the first advance of their army, George confided the defense of Semendra to his eldest son, Gregory, and taking with him his youngest son, Lazarus, he sought refuge at the court of the King of Hungary. The Prince of Wallachia, who either was unable to escape, or who remained, hoping to be victorious in the conflict, was taken, and imprisoned in the tower of Gallipoli. He was afterwards released, and sent back to Wallachia, upon renewing his oath of fidelity, and surrendering his two sons as hostages. In the meantime Amurat had laid siege to Semendra, which fell after a valiant and skilful defense. Gregory was made prisoner, had his eyes plucked out, and was transferred with his brother, who had been a long time held as a hostage at Adrianople, to the dungeons of Amasra and Tokat.

The Emperor, John II. Palæologus, fearing that his own empire would experience the same fate as Hungary and Servia, implored the assistance of the Latin princes against the Ottomans. He even revived the project of a union between the Churches, and contrary to the advice of his father, entertained the proposition of arranging with the Roman pontiff in a general council to be assembled beyond the Adriatic Sea. During the lifetime of Manuel, he had addressed, through the nuncio, Anthony Massan, envoy of Martin V., a letter to the Pope, testifying his desire to accomplish the union. "We would wish," he writes, "that the union could be made at once; but the nuncio is an eye-witness of our sad condition. We are nearly annihilated, our whole empire is exposed momentarily to the sword of the enemy, and it is not possible to assemble the bishops of Asia or Europe on account of the war with the infidels. As soon as God grants us peace, we shall write to you, and when we have received your answer, we wish the council to be convoked. We also beg you to pronounce excommunication against those of your communion who preserve peace with the infidels, and leave us alone in the contest against them. They should aid us, and not permit the vessels of the Mussulmans to be manned by Christians."

After the death of Martin V., the Greek monarch sent an embassy to his successor, Eugenius IV., begging him to carry out the intention of his predecessor, and call a council for the purpose of considering the union of the Greek and Latin Churches. The pontiff received the petition favorably, and promised to defray the expenses of the Greeks both in going to and returning from the council. Eugenius IV., having selected Ferrara as the place for the sessions of the council, sent money and galleys equipped at Venice and the isle of Candia, to convey the emperor and his suite to Italy. Palæologus, recalling the advice of Manuel, hesitated, but finally determined to embark. After a fatiguing voyage of seventy-seven days, they cast anchor before Venice (February 8, 1438). The following day the doge and senators, with numerous attendants, went to offer their homage to Palæologus, whom they found seated on a rich throne placed on the deck of the vessel. The sea was covered with gondolas hung with drapery of brilliant colors, the air resounded to the ringing of bells, the music of various instruments and the joyous acclamations of the innumerable spectators; the vessels, bearing the united flags of Rome and Venice, were rich with silk and gold. It would be difficult to describe the astonishment of the Greek monarch and his attendants as they ascended the grand canal, and saw for the first time the most beautiful city of the Christian world. They contemplated with admiration its marble palaces arising from the midst of the water, the hangings suspended from the Gothic windows, the banners floating above the doors, and the immense population of Venice the Superb; but their hearts were saddened upon beholding the spoils formerly taken by the Latins from Constantinople.

Being informed of the arrival of the emperor at Venice, the Pope deputed the Cardinal Sainte-Croix to welcome him to Italy. On the 28th of February Palæologus left Venice for Ferrara, where he was treated with all the honors formerly accorded to the emperors of the East.

The Marquis d' Este, accompanied by a number of cardinals and other prelates, received him outside the city gates. He made his entry upon a black horse magnificently caparisoned, whilst a white horse of great beauty, with crimson velvet housing and jewelled harness, was led before him. Over his head was borne a canopy supported by the children and nearest relatives of the Marquis. Thus he proceeded to the palace of the Pope, who met him at the door of his apartment, embraced him paternally, and conducted him to a seat by his side. After a short conversation, Eugenius IV. sent him with the same pomp to the palace which had been prepared for his use, and where he was treated during his stay with royal magnificence.

Three days later, the patriarch Joseph, who had remained at Venice, arrived with a portion of the metropolitans and bishops; but the sessions of the council were delayed four months in order to give time to the Latin princes and prelates to reach Ferrara.

Palæologus, with a number of his favorite courtiers, passed this interval in a large monastery agreeably situated six miles from Ferrara. Forgetting in the pleasures of the chase the calamities of his empire, he occupied himself in destroying game. The plague having made its appearance in Ferrara, the Pope proposed to transfer the council to Florence, which was accordingly done. It was in this city that the Greek prelates, with the exception of Mark of Ephesus, signed the act of union between the Greek and Latin Churches. The last session of the council was held in July, 1439, with great solemnity, in the Cathedral of Florence, and in it was proclaimed the decree of union, in the form of a bull by Eugenius IV., which was signed by the Pope, the emperor, and a large number of Greek and Latin prelates.

In the meantime, the patriarch Joseph had died suddenly, and Eugenius IV. urged the Greeks to elect, before their departure, a successor to the See of Constantinople. But the emperor and prelates were unwilling to accede to the proposition, saying that the election should necessarily take place in the cathedral of Saint Sophia. As the Greeks determined upon an immediate departure, the Pope gave generously far more than he had pledged himself for defraying their expenses. On the 26th of August John Palæologus left Florence for Venice, in which city he remained some time, and embarked only in October upon the galleys which had been furnished by the Pope to convey himself and his attendants to Constantinople, where he arrived the 1st of February, 1440.

On landing at Byzantium, he was saluted, or rather assailed, by the murmurs of the clergy and people. For two years the capital had been deprived of its civil and ecclesiastical rulers, and anarchy in every department was the consequence. Before his departure for Italy, the emperor had raised the hopes of his subjects by promises of speedy and powerful aid. But disappointed in their expectation, they openly expressed their indignation, and broke out into bitter invectives against the prelates who had signed the decree of union. This outburst of popular feeling was not without influence over the prelates, and nearly all of them retracted. Mark of Ephesus, who had refused adhesion, was regarded as the sole defender of his country.

In order to stifle the flame of religious discord, the emperor determined to bring about an election of a patriarch to supply the place of Joseph. The choice fell upon Metrophanes of Cyzica, who was consecrated in the church of Saint Sophia, and who took possession of the See in August. Having accomplished this, the emperor, either fearing to irritate Amurat, who was jealous of the apparent good feeling existing between the Greeks and the Latins, or losing all hope of aid from the West, showed no further zeal in the cause, and the Greek Church remained as before, independent of the Latin Church.

CHAPTER VI.

HUNNIADES AND SCANDERBEG.

Siege of Belgrade by the Ottomans—Successful defence of the city—John Hunniades—Defeat of the Mezidbeg—Battle of Vasag—The Ottomans conquered at Missa—Hunniades enters Buda in triumph—Peace of Segeddin, which is violated by the Christians—Battle of Varna—Amurat is induced to leave his retreat in Magnesia by the revolt of the Janizaries—Conquest of Peloponnesus—Battle of Kossova—Flight of John Hunniades—Defection and success of Scanderbeg—Amurat forced to raise the siege of Croïa—Death of John II. Palæologus—Demetrius disputes the throne with his brother, Constantine XII. Dragoses, emperor of Constantinople—Death of Amurat II.—Embassy of Phranza.

WHILST meditating upon the last blow which was to be dealt against the empire of Byzantium, Amurat, master of Servia, and aided by the despot of Wallachia, marched against the Hungarians, who, after the sudden death of Albert (1439), had been suffering the horrors of a civil war. Some called to the throne Ladislaus, king of Poland, upon the condition that he would marry Queen Elizabeth; others expoused the cause of Elizabeth, who, having no hope of being able to resist the Poles, had fled with her infant son to Austria, carrying with her the crown of Saint Stephen. Amurat took advantage of these discussions to besiege Belgrade, the outpost of Catholic Christendom. He confided the expedition to Alibeg, the son of Eurenos. On every elevated point in the vicinity, and on a hundred vessels on the Danube, he placed machines of all kinds for hurling stones. Hitherto, the sultan had marched with rapidity towards the aim he had in view, always victorious, and never arrested by any obstacle which impeded his progress. Before Belgrade, his star paled for the first time. His lieutenant found a worthy adversary in the prior Towan of Ragusa. The city repulsed successfully the repeated attacks of the besiegers. At the end of six months the king of Poland sent Lenziczky as an envoy to demand of the sultan to withdraw from Belgrade. Amurat, who intended to retire, replied nevertheless with pride that sooner or later he would conquer the city.

The vigorous defense of Belgrade was the prelude of the many defeats experienced by the Mussulmans at the hands of the celebrated John Hunniades, known by them under the name of *Yamko* (in Turkish, echo). John Corvinus, lord of Hunniades, was a magnate renowned for his courage. Descended from a noble family of Transylvania, he commanded, at the commencement of his career, twelve knights in the pay of the bishop of Tagrad; later, he accompanied Sigismund to Italy, and served in the army of Philip Mary Visconti. Upon his return to Hungary, he received from Sigismund the domain of Hunniades, situated on the confines of Transylvania and Wallachia. He increased his possessions by marrying a wealthy woman of illustrious birth. When Ladislaus entered Hungary he held the office of vaivode of Transylvania. He espoused the cause of this prince, who was called upon to defend his new kingdom against the simultaneous attacks of Elizabeth and the Turks. Under the modest title of the "White Knight of Wallachia" he acquired a brilliant renown. In the excess of their admiration, the Hungarians applied to him the words of the gospel: "*There was a man sent by God, whose name was John.*" In the eyes of the Turks, the old heroes of the Crusades were revived in this man, and they surnamed him the *Devil*. They never succeeded in entering the kingdom which he protected, and they wept for his death, because they would never have it in their power to avenge the humiliating defeats they had experienced in their contests with him. This Christian warrior had delivered Hungary from civil strife and foreign wars; ten times he combatted the infidels in pitched battles; fourteen times he surprised and dispersed their army. Defeated twice, Hunniades abandoned the victory only after an obstinate resistance. His brilliant exploits were a fortunate diversion for Constantinople. But for him, not only Hungary, but Bavaria, Germany, indeed all Christendom, would have been subjected to the Mussulman power. The King of Poland said of him, that he won the admiration of all without exciting the envy of any. Popes sent ambassadors to him as to a king.

In 1442 Mezidbeg entered Transylvania, and in the name of the sultan laid siege to Hermanstadt. Urged to take part in the war by the despot of Servia and his son Lazarus, who had sought refuge in Hungary after the death of Albert, Ladislaus and Hunniades determined to attack the Turks. Hunniades marched with his brave troops to the relief of the besieged city, and completely routed the Ottomans, who fled, leaving twenty thousand dead on the field of battle. The pasha and his son were among the slain. Hunniades, who had lost only three thousand men, crossed the mountains, entered Wallachia, and ravaged both shores of the Danube. The Hungarian general was received in triumph by his fellow citizens, so unaccustomed hitherto to any success in contests with the Turks; he sent to George Brankovich, as a trophy of his victory, a wagon so heavily laden with spoils that ten oxen could scarcely draw it. The heads of Mezidbeg and his son surmounted the whole, and an old Mussulman was deputed to offer the booty to the despot of Servia.

To avenge this defeat, Amurat prepared a formidable invasion, and ordered Sciabadin Pasha to march against the conqueror with the most efficient of the Janizaries, and an army amounting to eighty thousand men. He was also directed to punish the Wallachians and Moldavians, whom the White Knight had enticed from their alliance with the Ottomans. Sciabadin, in his pride, boasted that at the mere sight of his turban the enemy would take flight. Hunniades advanced to meet him with a force of only fifteen thousand, but all determined either to conquer or to die. The brave Hungarian answered the boasting of the pasha by a victory even more striking than his former triumph. Sciabadin was taken prisoner with five thousand men, and he lost two hundred standards. Amurat's best officers fell on the bloody field of Vasag. The sultan, humiliated as he was by this second defeat, still demanded from the Hungarians either the city of Belgrade or the payment of tribute. John Corvin advised an attack upon the sultan's States in punishment of this audacity, and Ladislaus, being also urged to war by the dethroned despot of Servia, was not unwilling to unite the Hungarian and Polish armies against the common enemy.

The following year (1443) was remarkable for the rapidity of the successes of Hunniades. A campaign of five months sufficed for him to win five battles and obtain possession of as many cities; the Hungarians, proud of the exploits of their general, named it the *long campaign*. This was the brilliant commencement of the crusade planned by the efforts of Cardinal Julian, legate of Eugenius IV:, who had sounded the alarm against the infidels. Never, since the fatal battle of Nicopolis, had so many different nations of Christian Europe united to combat the enemy of their faith. The army which crossed the Danube near Semendra on the 22d of July, under the command of Brankovich, was composed of Germans, Poles, Wallachians, Servians and Hungarians. Hunniades, at the head of twelve thousand valiant troops, entered Servia and ravaged the country as far as Nissa, whilst King Ladislaus and Cardinal Julian followed in two days with twenty thousand men. On the 3d of November, 1443, the Ottoman and Hungarian armies met near Nissa. Mussulman bravery was destined to be foiled by the skilful plans of Hunniades. Amurat was compelled to retreat precipitately beyond Mount Hemus, having lost two thousand men killed, nine standards, and four thousand made prisoners. Soon after the important city of Sophia surrendered.

A month later the Christian general fought another battle in the defiles of the Balkan, where his soldiers were obliged to contend not only with the enemy, but also to defend themselves against the avalanches and enormous masses of rocks and ice which dashed down the side of the mountain. They were, however, victorious, as they were in a subsequent battle, the only one in which King Ladislaus was present. Among the prisoners who fell into the hands of the crusaders was Mahmoud-Tchelebi, brother of the grand vizier, and son-in-law of Amurat. Hunniades recrossed the Danube with his army and entered Buda in triumph. Eugenius IV., the Genoese, the Venetians, and the duke of Burgundy sent ambassadors to Ladislaus, and Corvinus was treated with marked honor. All urged the continuation of the war and promised aid.' John Palæologus was also anxious for another expedition, hoping, by that means, to be permanently rid of the Turks. The despot of Servia and Cardinal Julian added their entreaties, each for his own particular interest. But the Poles opposed the undertaking in the most decided manner, because Poland was agitated by domestic dissensions and attacked from without by the Tartars. Besides, a portion of Hungary was still held by the Bohemians, who professed to support the cause of Ladislaus the Posthumous, but who desolated the northern provinces by their brigandage.

As Ladislaus himself desired the war, he gave orders to Corvinus to make the necessary preparations. Pope Eugenius, in concert with the Venetians and Genoese, assembled at Gaëta seventy galleys, the command of which was given to a Florentine cardinal named Francis Gondolmieri. This fleet sailed towards the Hellespont. It was destined to bar the passage of the Turks into Europe. The prince of Caramania had, for the third time, asserted his freedom from Ottoman rule, and he was resisting successfully the forces brought against him in Asia. Amurat attacked without respite on all sides, and wearied by defeat, pardoned the rebel, and with the view of putting an end to the disastrous war which he was waging in the northwest of his empire, he restored Wallachia to the vaivode Drakul; returned to George Brankovich his two sons, whose eyes had been plucked out, and surrendered the forts he had taken from him. Next he sent an ambassador to Hunniades to negotiate a peace. The affair was referred to the diet assembled at Segeddin, and the diet agreed to treat with the Ottomans. A truce of ten years was concluded in the presence of Cardinal Julian, who with difficulty concealed his discontent (12 July, 1444). The subjects of Ladislaus and George, on the contrary, were overjoyed. Amurat agreed to restore Servia and Herzegovina to Brankovich, to leave Wallachia under the suzerainty of the Hungarians, and to pay seventy thousand ducats for the ransom of his son-in-law. The Turks made oath upon the Koran, the Christians upon the Bible. The treaty was written in the two languages.

In the midst of the negotiations with the Christians, the sultan was plunged in the deepest grief by the news of the death of his eldest son, Aleaddin. Amurat, who united to great military talents a tender affection for his children, was so keenly affected by this loss, that he determined to abdicate the throne. Selecting from his ministers those who had grown old in his service, and who were most able to guide his inexperienced son, then only fourteen years of age, he resigned in his favor and retired to Magnesia with a small number of favorite courtiers.

But whilst the sultan thus placed the reins of government in the hands of a boy, the enemies of the Ottoman empire were eagerly watching a favorable opportunity to take revenge for all the disasters inflicted on them by the Mussulman arms. Scarcely had the truce been signed, when deputies arrived from the fleet of the crusaders with assurances that it was not possible for the army of the infidels to pass from Asia into Europe. They urged Ladislaus to act promptly. The emperor, John II. Palæologus, fearing that the truce of Segeddin might prove disadvantageous to himself, solicited from the Pope, from the Franks and Philip of Burgundy, a new crusade which might efface the disgrace of Nicopolis. The Hungarians regretted having lost the opportunity of driving the Turks from Europe, and Cardinal Julian was no less impatient to terminate the war against the enemies of Christ; he therefore took advantage of circumstances to break the treaty. To secure the co-operation of George, he was promised additional territory. The Poles were discontented because the Russians were at that very time invading Lithuania.

The second expedition from Bulgaria commenced by the passage of the Danube at Orsowa. This time, instructed by the experience of the former campaign, they resolved to push on directly to Gallipoli. Two roads conducted thither: one between Mount Hemus and the sea, longer and more secure; the other through the mountains, straight, but steep and difficult. Ladislaus selected the former, after having made an unsuccessful attack upon Nicopolis. A Wallachian chief, seeing the small number of men under his command, urged him to retreat; but Ladislaus persisted in his advance, and encamped near Varna, a city situated on the banks of the sea.

In consideration of the extreme danger, Amurat consented to leave his solitude in Magnesia; and indignant at the violation of the treaty, he hastened from Asia, at the head of an army of forty thousand men. Instead of going to the Hellespont, where lay the fortified fleet, he landed on the shores of the Bosphorus. Genoese vessels transported his troops, upon receiving in payment a ducat for every man. From Adrianople he proceeded by forced marches, and encamped not far from the Hungarians. Cardinal Julian wished to fortify their camp, but Hunniades and the despot of Servia opposed the plan, and they determined to give battle to the Turks.

The eve of November 11, 1444, the troops on both sides placed themselves in order of battle. Hunniades directed the arrangement of the Christians. The contest commenced at day-dawn. Cardinal Julian and George Brankovich made the first attack upon the Turks. They were repulsed; but Hunniades and Ladislaus restored order, and performed prodigies of valor. The sultan, seeing his Janizaries giving way before the enemy, held up a copy of the treaty made with the Hungarians, and, lifting his eyes to heaven, prayed the God of the Christians to punish their perjury. Ladislaus, carried away by his enthusiasm, rushed into the midst of the Janizaries. Surrounded by five hundred cavaliers, his body-guard, under the banner of Saint George, borne by Stephen of Bathori, he dealt death wherever he passed, and sought particularly to reach Amurat. But his horse was wounded in the foot by a lance, and fell, throwing his rider to the ground. An old Janizary cut off his head before he had time to recover himself, and placing it upon the point of a lance, held it aloft, crying to the enemy: "Behold the head of your king."

This horrible pendant to another lance, upon which the sultan had suspended the treaty of Segeddin as a monument of Christian perfidy, dismayed the Hungarians, and caused their defeat. They retreated precipitately, notwithstanding the efforts made by Hunniades to recover the body of the young king. The hero was himself obliged to yield, and recognizing the divine vengeance in the disaster, he retired from the field. The Hungarians lost two-thirds of their army, including Cardinal Julian, the author of their misfortunes, and Stephen Bathori, father of the vaivode of Transylvania. Thirty thousand Ottomans were slain. Two hundred and fifty wagons loaded with valuable articles fell into the hands of the victors. The sultan announced his success to the sultan of Egypt, and to make known to him what men he had conquered, he sent him twenty-five breastplates taken from Hungarian nobles. The head of Ladislaus was sent to the governor of Brusa.

George and Hunniades recrossed the Danube with

the remains of the army of the crusaders, who were not pursued by the Turks. Great was the grief in Hungary, in Poland, and throughout Christendom. The people mourned the death of Ladislaus, and the sultan erected a column on the spot where he fell; but the modest inscription praised his valor, and deplored his misfortune, without condemning his imprudence.

Satisfied with having saved the state, and weary of the throne, Amurat resigned his crown a second time, and retired to his charming retreat in Magnesia. But again his repose was interrupted, and the empire claimed his services. The Janizaries revolted, and by their disorders spread terror throughout the city of Adrianople. The ministers of the young sultan decided to beg the assistance of Amurat. Sacrificing his pleasures to the wishes of his former subjects, this prince returned to Adrianople, and, for the third time, assumed the sceptre. The Janizaries acknowledged the voice of their master, and submitted at once to his authority, so great was the fear and respect inspired by his name.

Once more in possession of the sovereign power, which he wielded until his death, Amurat turned his attention to the northern portion of the ancient empire of Byzantium in Europe, of Peloponnesus, and Albania. Shortly after the disaster of Varna, in which the Latins alone had borne the penalty of the perfidy, he had renewed the truce with the emperor, whose states were then limited to the territory surrounding the capital, and included within the long wall of Anastasa. The treaty which he had signed did not comprehend his brothers, the despots of

Peloponnesus. Theodore had been appointed despot of Sparta at the division of the empire between the sons of Manuel. He was succeeded, at his death, by his nephew, Theodore, son of Andronicus, who afterwards exchanged his dominions with his uncle, Constantine. This prince succeeded in extending his sway over the whole peninsula, excepting that portion belonging to his brother Thomas. The progress of Constantine, who was destined to ascend the throne of Byzantium, was materially aided by the long campaign of Hunniades.

This increase of power provoked the envy and attacks of Amurat. His own desire, and the entreaties of the beglerbey of Roumelia, and the duke of Athens, Neri Acciaiuoli, who had broken his alliance with Constantine, induced him to undertake an expedition against Greece. Leaving the Emperor of Constantinople in peace, he made a descent upon central Greece at the head of sixty thousand men. At Thebes he received the homage of the Florentine prince, Neri; thence he proceeded to force the wall which Constantine had built at the isthmus of Hexamilon, and behind which he had intrenched himself with his brother Thomas and all the forces of the Peloponnesus (1446). Corinth, being abandoned by its garrison, which was engaged in the defense of the wall, became the prey of the barbarians and was delivered to the flames. For the fourth time the fortifications of the isthmus were destroyed and the trenches filled up. The devastation of Patras, the second capital of Morea, followed the burning of Corinth. At the approach of the Turks the greater part of the inhabitants had taken flight;

four thousand remained, and they expiated their blind confidence by the loss of their liberty. The Janizaries commenced by mining the walls of the citadel, which made a vigorous resistance. But the Greeks, pouring down streams of boiling pitch, forced them to withdraw, and then filled up the breaches and fortified themselves anew. When the remainder of his army arrived, the sultan raised the siege and concluded with Constantine a treaty, in virtue of which Peloponnesus was to be tributary to the Turks. Sixty thousand Greeks were reduced to slavery. Constantine as despot of Sparta, and his brother Thomas as despot of Achaia, were obliged to pay a capitation tax for all the subjects whom it pleased the conqueror to leave them.

That Amurat did not consummate the ruin of the Greeks after the devastation of Peloponnesus, was due to his ignorance of the Hungarian character. He did not comprehend that his victories had served only to animate their courage, and that he would derive a small advantage from them and at a great sacrifice. Consequently, he employed his forces in harassing Hungary, being favored, as he supposed, by the difficulties surrounding Hunniades. Appointed regent during the minority of the young king, Ladislaus the Posthumous, who was detained at his court by Frederic III., Hunniades during two years ravaged Austria, Styria and Carinthia; the two following years he employed in contests with the Turks, and in appeasing domestic discords. The wisdom of his administration proved that he united the talents of the statesman to those of the warrior. Appeals made to him were attended to at whatever time or in whatever place they were presented, and his spirit of conciliation and prudence soon put an end to civil dissensions. He was a scourge to the Emperor of Germany, who refused to restore to the Hungarians their young king and the crown of St. Stephen, which had been placed in his hands by Elizabeth. In the midst of these various cares and duties, he did not neglect to keep a watchful eye upon the Turks; by day his guards were ever on the alert, by night he kindled large fires to prevent a surprise, and thus the enemy were unable to cross the Danube.

Four years after the battle of Varna, Hunniades resolved no longer to limit the war to defensive operations, but to take active measures against Amurat. Accordingly, he made an alliance with the Prince of Albania, Scanderbeg, and placed himself at the head of the finest and best disciplined army which had yet been raised in Hungary; it numbered eighty thousand men, including eight thousand Wallachians under Dan, who had been appointed vaivode in place of Drakul, and two thousand German and Bohemian arquebusiers. Hunniades crossed the Danube, in order to make a junction with Scanderbeg, and invaded Servia. Through his assistance, the Despot George Brankovich recovered his principality; but terrified by the power of the Turks, and jealous of the Hungarian hero, he not only refused the auxiliaries demanded by the Christian army, but he perfidiously betrayed to the sultan the plans of Hunniades.

Upon receiving information of this invasion, Amurat hastened to the assistance of his ally, the despot, prevented the junction of the armies of Corvinus and Scanderbeg, and met the Hungarian army in the plain of Kossora, memorable for the victory gained fifty-nine years before by Amurat I. The Christians encamped there in October. The Ottoman army, a hundred and fifty thousand strong, employed three days in crossing the Stitnitza, a river running through the plain. Confiding too implicitly in his good fortune, Hunniades, instead of waiting for the arrival of the troops promised him by the Prince of Albania, left his camp and advanced to meet the enemy, near the village of Brod. Before accepting battle, the sultan made overtures, hoping to come to terms, but they were rejected by the haughty Hunniades.

On the eve of the 17th of October, the two armies took their position. For three days the skilful arrangements of the Hungarian general, his heavy cavalry, the universal hatred of the Turks, and the hope of aid from Scanderbeg, counterbalanced the superiority of numbers, which was fearfully disproportionate. The plain, which was five miles wide, could not contain the solid front of the Turkish army. Their meals were taken on the field of battle. The second day victory still hung in the balance, when the Hungarians were betrayed by the Wallachians, who deserted to the Ottomans. They were, in consequence, forced to give way, but they retired in good order and gained their intrenchments. Despairing of success, Hunniades left the camp secretly with a few officers. The following day the Hungarian army performed prodigies of valor; but being abandoned by their chief, they disbanded and were massacred. Seventeen thousand lay dead upon the field; among them were many magnates of Hungary and the brother of Corvinus. Amurat's loss amounted to thirty-four thousand; he ordered the greater part of the bodies to be thrown into the Stitnitza.

Hunniades encountered many perils in his flight: two Turks seized him, but whilst they were disputing the possession of his gold cross he recovered his sword, killed one of his assailants, and put the other to flight. He afterwards fell into the hands of his enemy, the despot George, at Semendra. He obtained his release upon condition that his son Matthias should marry the daughter of George; his son Ladislaus Corvinus, was to be retained as a hostage. Hunniades soon liberated his son by force of arms and compelled George to submission. Amurat, furious that the despot had not delivered the Hungarian general into his hands, ordered his states to be invaded. Corvinus surprised the Turkish army and completely routed it. From this time until his death, Amurat left Hungary in peace. Hunniades' entire attention was given to the affairs of his own kingdom and of Austria, until he gained his most renowned, but also his last victory over the Ottomans, at the famous siege of Belgrade. The defeats of Varna and Kossora only temporarily obscured the glory which the hero had acquired in his combats with the infidels. The too great confidence inspired by his former success was, no doubt, the cause of the reverses he experienced.

A contemporary of John Hunniades, his rival in glory, great in his struggles against the Ottoman power, and in the heroic defence of his country, now appears in the arena. A generous athlete for the freedom of his country, he demands our attention by occupying the Mussulman armies in such a manner as to delay the ruin of the Greek empire. George Castriot, the youngest son of John Castriot, prince of Albania and tributary to Amurat, had been left, as we have said, a hostage with his three brothers in the hands of his suzerain. The latter mingled without distinction amid the throng of slaves on duty in the palace, and died young. George, left alone, attracted the attention and won the affection of the sultan by his uncommon intellect, his firm character, and fine appearance; he was educated in the religion of Mahomet. He surpassed all his companions in his skill, strength and courage, which rendered him, at eighteen years of age, the most redoubtable warrior in the army. With one blow he cleft the head of a bull; he had leaped alone within the walls of a besiged city. Three successive victories, over a Tartar and two Persians who had challenged the Ottoman warriors, gained him the favor of Amurat, the surname of *Scanderbeg* (prince Alexander), the title and rank of *sanjakbeg*, the command of five thousand horse, and opened to him the way to the highest dignities in the empire. But upon the death of John Castriot, the sultan, instead of restoring to Scanderbeg the principality of Albania, where his father had reigned, appointed a governor, and was particular in keeping the young prince always engaged in war. Wounded by the injustice, and burning with the desire of breaking his chains, Scanderbeg resolved to avenge himself upon the first favorable opportunity. Therefore, when the Turks were beaten by Hunniades near Nissa, during the long campaign, George Castriot, then twenty-nine years of age, deserted the flag of Amurat. In the confusion of the defeat, dagger in hand, he forced the reis-effendi, or principal secretary, to deliver to him a firman, ordering the governor of Croïa to resign the command of the place to the bearer of the message, as his successor. Lest too prompt a discovery might prevent the accomplishment of his designs, he stabbed the innocent accomplice of his artifice, and made his escape with his nephew, Hamsa (1443).

Seven days after leaving the Turkish army, Castriot, in virtue of the order signed by the reis-effendi, obtained possession of Croïa, introduced during the night six hundred men who had joined him during his flight, and massacred the sleeping garrison. Complete success having thus crowned his bold stratagem, Scanderbeg publicly renounced the prophet and the sultan, proclaimed himself the avenger of his nation and his family, and called upon the people to combat for their liberty. His relatives possessed many cities in Epirus; they hastened to join his standard, and to concert with the successful Scanderbeg the means of throwing off the yoke of the Ottomans. The names of religion and liberty caused a general revolt; Petrella, Petralba and Stelusia acknowledged the new master of Epirus, and he soon recovered the whole of his paternal inheritance. The princes of the neighboring states united with him, and in an assembly of all the states of Epirus, he was chosen generalissimo to conduct the war against the Turks; the allies pledged themselves to furnish their contingent of men and money, and the brave Albanians swore to live and die with their hereditary prince. Affable in his manners, severe in military discipline, the *soldier of Christ* banished vice from his camp, and maintained his authority over his intrepid companions by giving a good example. Under the guidance of such a chief, the Albanians believed themselves invincible, and they inspired their enemies with the most exalted idea of their valor. Attracted by his fame, the bravest adventurers of France and Germany ranged themselves under the banner of Scanderbeg, in order to share his perils and his glory. Eight thousand cavalry and seven thousand infantry composed the regular army of the hero of Albania who, for twenty-three years, resisted with this small force the whole power of the Ottoman empire, and the efforts of two dreaded sultans, Amurat II. and his son.

Having by his address and courage regained the states of his father, and celebrated the baptism of his nephew, Hamsa, who was as eager as himself to defend the faith of his ancestors, Scanderbeg, ever active and watchful, collected his forces and encamped near Croïa, which was admirably defended by its position on a rock and by its strong walls, and which possessed large stores of ammunition Here he awaited the Turkish general, Ali Pasha, who had been sent against him with forty thousand men. The skilful disposition of his troops gave him great advantage, as they were able from the steep rocks over which they were distributed to mow down the enemy with artillery, the latter being crowded in a kind of valley encircled by the chain of mountains. According to the account given by Barletius, twenty-two thousand Turks fell in this first engagement, two thousand were made prisoners, and twenty-four standards were captured, whilst the victors lost only one hundred men (1443).

The abdication of Amurat after the campaign of Hungary procured a short repose for Scanderbeg; but new combats soon presented him with new fields for acquiring glory. He successively defeated Firouz-Pacha and Mustapha-Pasha, drove them from Epirus, and laid siege to Daïna, a fortress of which the Venetians had taken possession. The approach of an Ottoman army, however, obliged Scanderbeg to raise the siege and make peace with Venice. Mustapha did not succeed in effacing the disgrace of his first defeat; conquered a second time, he left ten thousand dead on the field, and was made prisoner with ten Turkish officers of distinction; the sultan ransomed them for twenty-five thousand ducats.

To avenge these humiliating defeats of his generals, Amurat resolved to conduct the army in person. More than a hundred thousand men advanced under his command to conquer Sfetigrad and Dibra (1449). On the 14th of May he appeared before the former of these cities; it was forced to capitulate, notwithstanding the heroic courage of Scanderbeg, who unceasingly harassed the besiegers, and who killed Firouz-Pasha with his own hand. Dibra was defended with admirable constancy by its commander, Parlat, but it was conquered by an artifice and the superstitious scruples of the inhabitants: a dead dog was thrown into the only well in the city, and the people refused to drink the water. In this campaign, Amurat lost more than twenty thousand men of his best troops. After the departure of the Turks, Scanderbeg besieged Sfetigrad for a month, but without success.

In the spring of the following year, Amurat returned to besiege Croïa in person. Scanderbeg placed the women and children with his allies, the Venetians. Yielding to the superior numbers of the enemy, he retreated to the Tumenistos, an inaccessible mountain about a mile from the capital. The sultan located his camp in the plain of Tyana, and appeared before the walls the latter part of April. The faithful Uracontes had been appointed to the command of the city; Amurat, having in vain tried to win him over, ordered several cannon to be cast; in a fortnight he had ten, four of which threw immense masses of rock, and the other six, stones of a less size. Scanderbeg allowed the Ottoman artillery to batter down a portion of the wall, and he met the assault with the close ranks of the Albanians, which formed an impenetrable rampart. Several times during the siege, the indefatigable warrior, emerging during the night from the gorges of the mountains, surprised the enemy buried in sleep, and made a frightful carnage. On one occasion eight thousand Turks were slain. The besieged, under the command of their governor, Uracontes, made frequent sorties, spread terror among the Janizaries, and added to the disorder occasioned by the nocturnal expeditions of their prince. At last, tired of these inglorious skirmishes, which were daily weakening his army, Amurat sent an ambassador to Scanderbeg, offering him the investiture of the revolted provinces, provided he would acknowledge himself a vassal of the sultan, and would agree to pay a tribute of five or ten thousand ducats. The ambassador, Youssouf, accompanied by some of the inhabitants of Dibra, vainly sought the Albanian chief, for two days, on the Tumenistos and the banks of the Ismos; at last he found him in the *Red Camp*, about an hour's journey from the river. Scanderbeg rejected the proposition of the sultan, who, being compelled to raise the siege, retired ill and humiliated towards Adrianople. Before reaching his destination, he suffered many losses in the defiles of the mountains, being constantly harassed by an almost invisible enemy. The Ottoman troops entered their winter quarters with the shame of having been constantly vanquished by an army far less numerous than their own, but composed of people determined to die free and faithful to the religion of Christ.

During the winter which passed between the surrender of Sfetigrad and the siege of Coria, John Palæologus died, leaving the Greek Church in a state of agitation, and his empire in a deplorable condition: the Turkish power was formidable, his subjects extremely weak, and his family were divided by a fatal discord (1449). The death of Andronicus and the monastic profession of Isidore, had reduced the royal family to the three sons of Manuel, Constantine, Demetrius and Thomas. As the last sovereign left no children, the throne belonged to

Constantine, who was in the Morea with Thomas. Demetrius, possessed of the domain of Selymbria, was in the vicinity of the capital, at the head of numerous partisans. The ambition of this prince did not abate in view of the calamities which menaced the empire. The obsequies of John Palæologus were performed with extraordinary and suspicious precipitation. In order to justify his pretensions to the crown, Demetrius observed that he was the eldest son born after his father ascended the throne. But the senate and soldiers, the empress mother, and the despot Thomas, the clergy and the people, unanimously maintained the right of the legitimate successor, Constantine Dragoses, a mild and just prince, possessed of a great and noble soul, and deficient neither in talents nor courage.

Amurat had the gratification of fixing the order of succession to the throne, as if he were the arbiter of the empire. The grand-chamberlain, Phranza, was sent to Adrianople in quality of ambassador. The sultan received with benignity the petition of Phranza, dismissed him with valuable gifts, and confirming the choice of the majority of the Greeks, he secured to the legitimate heir that sceptre which his own son was soon to break in the hands of the last of the Palæologi. Constantine XII was crowned by two illustrious deputies, in the ancient city of Lycurgus and Leonidas. The new emperor left Morea in the spring, and entered his capital amid the acclamations of his subjects. He celebrated his accession with brilliant festivals, and his largesses exhausted the treasury. Pardoning the ambition of his brother Demetrius, he bestowed upon him and Thomas his states of Peloponnesus.

Towards the end of 1450 Amurat celebrated at Adrianople the marriage of his son Mahomet with the daughter of a Turcoman prince. Soon after the departure of the prince to Magnesia, of which he was governor, the sultan was struck with apoplexy at a banquet (1451). During his long reign he had been just to his subjects and firm. Even the Greeks acknowledged that he faithfully kept his word, that he was moderate in prosperity, and that he never refused peace to the vanquished who asked it.

In the meantime the new emperor was occupied with the choice of a wife. The daughter of the doge of Venice was proposed to him; but how could an hereditary monarch, the successor of the Roman Cæsars, from an alliance with the daughter of an elective magistrate? The difference in rank was too great; such, at least, was the opinion of the Byzantine nobles. Next, Constantine hesitated between the royal families of Georgia and Trebizond; and the care of concluding this important affair was intrusted to the grand-chamberlain, Phranza. This officer left Constantinople empowered to act for the emperor and surrounded by all the pomp which became his high mission. The suite of the envoy was composed of nobles, guards, monks, physicians and musicians. Who could imagine that in the midst of the disorders of the Greek empire, this embassy was prolonged for two years? And yet Phranza asserts it as a fact.

Having arrived in Georgia, a country covered with ramifications of the Caucasus and filled with fertile and charming valleys, the Greeks were surprised to see the inhabitants of the cities and villages collect around them, and express the greatest delight upon hearing the harmonious sounds of the instruments, without knowing how they were produced. From this hospitable land, where the ambassador had been received with all the honor due his rank, he went to Trebizond; John IV. was then on the throne. Here he learned the recent death of the Ottoman sovereign. He was much grieved, for he clearly foresaw that Mahomet II,, young and ambitious, would not long adhere to the peace policy adopted by his father. After the death of Amurat, his widow Mary, a Christian, daughter of George, despot of Servia, had been loaded with honors and presents and permitted to return to her family. In consequence of Mary's reputation for merit and beauty, Phranza considered her the most suitable choice for the emperor, his master, although she was nearly fifty years of age. Constantine listened to the proposition transmitted him by Phranza; but his intentions were opposed by court factions, and Mary herself rendered the union impossible by bidding an irrevocable adieu to the world and retiring to a cloister. Phranza then gave the preference. to the princess of Georgia, whose father dazzled by so glorious an alliance, offered, contrary to the ancient custom of his nation, a dowry of fifty-six thousand ducats, besides an annual pension of five thousand, and a liberal recompense to the emperor's ambassador. Upon the return of Phranza, Constantine ratified the treaty and gave assurances to the deputies from Georgia, that in the spring he would send galleys to convey the future empress to Constantinople. Preparations were made during the winter for the embassy, but the young princess never saw her intended husband; all these projects were buried under the ruins of the empire.

CHAPTER VII.

PREPARATIONS FOR THE SIEGE OF CONSTANTINOPLE—CONSTERNATION OF THE GREEKS.

The sultan Mahomet II.—His character—Mahomet confims the peace with the ambassadors of Constantine—Hostile intentions of the sultan—He constructs a fortress on the Bosphorus—Embassy from Constantine to Mahomet—Reply of the sultan—Energy of the emperor—Commencement of hostilities—Devastation of Peloponnesus—Orban, a caster of cannons, deserts to the Turks—Constantine in vain implores aid from the West—State of Europe—Provisions carried to Constantinople—Picture of Constantinople.

THE conquest of Constantinople by the Ottomans was one of the most memorable events of the XV. Century: the fall of the throne of the Greek emperors after a duration of eleven hundred years, and the establishment of the Turkish empire on the soil of Europe, were circumstances too important not to exert a powerful influence over Christian nations. Therefore, the sultan who dealt the final blow against the ancient Byzantium, has obtained a celebrity in history surpassing that of any other sovereign of his dynasty.

Three days after the death of Amurat, his son Mahómet, who was at Magnesia, was informed of it by a courier dispatched for the purpose by Khalil-Pasha. Mahomet, then twenty-one years of age, eagerly replaced upon his brow the crown which his father had twice in his life-time resigned to him. No sooner had he received the news, than springing upon an Arabian charger, he exclaimed: "Let those who love me follow me!" He reached Gallipoli in two days, remained there two days to give his attendants time to precede him and notify the inhabitants of Adrionople of his arrival. The viziers and emirs, the imans and cadis, the soldiers, and the greater part of the people, met their new master outside the city. Having paid with all the nobles the last duties to his father, he admitted them to kiss his hand. The following day he took formal possession of the throne, in presence of the viziers and high officers of the empire. Ishak-Pasha and the grand vizier, Khald, remained at some distance. The latter, by whose advice Amurat had twice resumed the crown, had no reason to anticipate any cordiality from the young sultan. Mahomet confirmed him in his dignity. Ishak-Pasha, as governor of Anatolia, was charged with conveying the body of Amurat to Brusa.

Mahomet, who conceived from his contemporaries the surname of Conqueror, which title has been confirmed to him by posterity, had a full face, a thick beard and dark complexion; he was very robust, and able to support the fatigues of war, in which he was engaged during his whole life. He handled arms with uncommon dexterity. He was of a fiery temperament; he had a bright, penetrating mind, was subtle and crafty. This bold, energetic prince, insatiable in his thirst for glory, was not indebted for his conquests solely to his courage, great as it was; his prudence and his policy were equal to his valor. He spoke five languages, Arabian, Persian, Chaldaïc, Latin and Greek. He had studied with success mathematics, astronomy and military tactics. History and geography were familiar to him; his emulation was aroused by reading the life and actions of the great men of antiquity. He encouraged science and arts, and he himself cultivated poetry and letters. But nothing could compensate for his contempt of all religion, his deliberate cruelty, the corruption of his heart, the ambition and love of pomp and pleasure which influenced all his actions, his disregard for his plighted word, his violation of treaties confirmed by the most solemn oaths, his licentiousness and excesses of every kind, but above all the fratricide by which he disgraced the commencement of his reign.

Ambassadors from Asia and Europe were promptly sent to Adrianople to congratulate the successor of Amurat II. upon his accession to the throne, and to solicit his friendship. Among them were the envoys of Constantine Drogoses and his brother, Demetrius, despot of Peloponnesus. Mahomet received them in the most gracious manner, expressed himself in moderate terms, and swore that, like his father, he would maintain peace. The sultan endeavored particularly to inspire with confidence the ambassador of the Greek emperor by flattering assurances, and by the solemn promise to consecrate the revenues of a rich domain lying on the banks of the Strymon to the payment of the annual pension for the support of Orkhan, whom the policy of the Palæologi retained a prisoner at Constantinople.

Notwithstanding these friendly assurances, Pope Nicholas V. foresaw what the religion of Christ would have to suffer from Mahomet; moved by the danger which menaced the greater part of the

Christian states, and particularly the Byzantine empire, he exhorted the sovereigns of Europe to aid the Greeks, and he endeavored to excite the zeal of the people. For this purpose he sent Cardinal Casa to Germany with the title of legate, with instructions to effect a firm peace between the princes, and to request the faithful to assist by their alms those who were exposed to the attacks of the Turks. At the same time he wrote to Constantine, informing him of the disposition of the Latins to aid him in the coming struggle.

In the meantime, Mahomet, having renewed an alliance with the envoys from Wallachia, Genoa, Galata, Chios, Mitylene, and the knights of Rhodes, and concluded a truce of three years with John Hunniades, marched in person against the prince of Caramania, who, in the hope of recovering the provinces of which he had been despoiled, had just revolted. But his attempt proved abortive, and in pledge of his submission, Ibrahim offered the hand of his daughter to the sultan. Mahomet accepted the proposition, being eager to execute the design he secretly meditated of conquering Constantinople.

An imprudent and unseasonable demand made by the Greek emperor furnished the son of Amurat with a pretext for the fatal rupture. During the campaign of Caramania, his ambassadors presented themselves in the Turkish camp, and complained, in the name of their sovereign, of the non-payment of the pension due for Orkhan; they most indiscreetly added a menace to liberate the prince and support his pretensions to the throne, if double the amount of the sum agreed upon were not paid immediately.

The grand vizier, Khalil, who was friendly to the Greeks, was, however, compelled to communicate to them his master's sentiments. "Foolish and miserable Romans," he said to them, "I have long penetrated your artifices and your crafty devices; our late supreme lord, Amurat II., a man of upright conscience and mild disposition, entertained the kindest feelings towards you; but the case is different with my present master, who is arrested in his designs by no obstacle. Should Constantinople escape his grasp, I shall believe that divine mercy defers for a time the chastisement of your intrigues and subterfuges. Madmen that you are! Scarcely is the treaty signed, when you come to Asia to terrify us with silly phantoms. We are not weak children, without experience. If you have the power to do aught against us, use it at once; release Orkhan, proclaim him sovereign of Thrace, call the Hungarians to your aid, recover from us the provinces we took from you long ago. But know that your plans will not succeed; you but provoke and precipitate your ruin. I shall inform my master of all that has passed, and he will order what seems best to him."

These terrible words of the vizier dismayed the ambassadors; but the sultan, although indignant at their audacity, still acted deceitfully, as the liberation of Orkhan might excite civil war in his empire. He reassured the Greeks by a cordial reception and expressions of good feeling, promising them to examine the case and do them justice as soon as he returned to Adrianople. But when he had crossed the Hellespont and entered Gallipoli, he expelled the Greeks from all the towns and villages on the Strymon, whence the revenues were derived for the payment of Orkhan's pension. He thus proclaimed his hostile intentions, and prepared to make the emperor expiate his imprudent menaces. A second order issued by the young sultan threatened, or even commenced, the siege of Byzantium.

Bajazet-Ilderim had constructed a fortress on the Asiatic shore of the Bosphorus. Mahomet conceived the design of elevating another directly opposite, on the European shore, thus securing to himself the command of the straits. Early in the winter he published throughout his empire an edict commanding a thousand masons and carpenters, with a sufficient number of lime-burners and hodmen, to repair in the spring to a place called Asomaton, not far from Constantinople, where he also ordered materials for the work to be forwarded. Upon receiving this news, the Christians of Asia, Thrace and the Islands were filled with the deepest sorrow, and in their sad forebodings they exclaimed: "The destruction of the city is nigh at hand; already we perceive the fatal signs of the ruin of the nation; the days of Antichrist are upon us! What shall we do? What will become of us? Rather let us die, O Lord, than see the sack of our city!"

Constantine Dragoses, justly alarmed, hastened to send ambassadors to the sultan, not to claim, as on the former occasion, the promised pension, but to dissuade him from the execution of his design. Being admitted to Mahomet's presence, they represented to him that his grandfather had begged of the emperor, Manuel, with the submission of a son to a father, the permission to build a fort on his own territory; and that the double fortification which he contemplated, and which would render the Turks masters of the Straits, could only have for its object an interruption of the alliance between the two nations; it would, moreover, interfere with the commerce of the Latins in the Black Sea, deprive Constantinople of the advantages to be derived from this, and perhaps even reduce the city to starvation. He begged the sultan, accordingly, to renounce the project and accept a tribute, promising to preserve for him a friendship as constant and inviolable as that which the Greeks had entertained towards his father.

"I am planning no enterprise against your city," replied the perfidious Mahomet, "but the walls which surround it form the limit of your empire. If I choose to construct a fort, have you a right to oppose me? Both shores belong to me: the Asiatic shore, because it is in the possession of the Mussulmans; the European, because the Christians are unable to defend it. Do you remember the danger incurred by my father when the Hungarian allies of the emperor were marching towards Thrace, and when the passage of the Hellespont was closed against him? He was compelled to force his way through the Bosphorus; but your means of injuring him did not correspond to your ill-will. I was then a child, and I remained at Adrianople, expecting the arrival of the Hungarians, who were ravaging the environs of Varna; the Mussulmans trembled, plunged in affliction, and the *gabours* (infidels), in the midst of prosperity and joy, laughed at their misfortunes. Amurat, my father, victor in the battle of Varna, made a vow to construct on the Bosphorus, on this very spot, a fortress opposite the one on the Asiatic shore. I will fulfil this vow, with the help of God. What right have you to prevent me from doing as I please on my own territory? Return to your homes, and say to your master that the present sovereign cannot compare with his predecessors; let him execute quickly what they were unable to do. If another envoy present himself as the bearer of similar messages, he shall be flayed alive."

When the ambassadors related at Constantinople the answer of the sultan, the city was in consternation. Constantine wished to take up arms at once, and prevent the Ottomans from establishing themselves on the Bosphorus. He was dissuaded from this course by the council of his ministers, who influenced him to adopt a less noble plan. They induced him to prove his patience by suffering additional injuries, to throw upon the Turks the crime of being the aggressors, to rely upon time and his good fortune for their defence, and for the destruction of a fortress of which the sultan could not long hold possession, standing, as it would, at the gates of a large and populous capital. Thus the winter passed; credulous men cherished vain hopes, men of wisdom entertained fears which proved but too well founded. The Greeks slept tranquilly on the edge of the abyss which was already gaping at their feet, until the return of spring and the approach of their dreaded enemy announced to them their destruction.

Towards the end of March, 1452, all the materials necessary for the construction of the fortress were carried, by sea and land, from Europe and Asia to the appointed place. The lime had been prepared in Cataphrygia; the forests of Nicomedia and Heraclea furnished the wood, and the stone was sent from the quarries of Anatolia. At the same time the plain of Asomaton was covered with workmen. Two laborers aided each of the thousand masons, of whom was required a certain daily amount of work. The sultan had adopted in the plan of the fort the whimsical idea of making it resemble, in form, the Arabian letters composing the name of Mahomet. Thus it rested on three towers; two near each other at the foot of the promontory, anciently called *Hermæum Promontorium;* and the third immediately on the sea. The walls were twenty-five feet thick; the towers were thirty in diameter. The whole edifice was covered with lead. Mahomet directed in person a portion of the work, and his three viziers, charged with superintending the rest, gave attention particularly to the towers. Animated by the presence of the sultan, the Ottomans displayed incredible ardor; men of all classes, even the highest dignitaries, mingled with the workmen and carried stones, mortar and bricks. In addition to the materials sent from Asia, the Mussulmans used the remains of several churches situated on the Bosphorus, among others the marble columns of the magnificent church dedicated to St. Michael, the archangel.

Terrified at the progress of a work which he was now powerless to arrest, the Greek emperor passed from useless threats to humble supplications. He sent an embassy to Mahomet, requesting a Turkish guard to protect the fields and harvests of his subjects dispersed throughout the valleys of the Bosphorus, and he daily sent him for his table costly wines and delicate viands. But neither the entreaties nor the attentions of Constantine appeased his implacable enemy. On the contrary, the sultan ordered horses and mules to be pastured on the lands of the Greeks, and directed any attack made by the natives to be repelled by force. The son of Isfendiar, son-in-law of the sultan, turned his horses to pasture in a field of ripe grain near Epibaton (now Birados). The injury inflicted on them irritated the Greeks, who undertook to drive out the animals. A Turkish groom struck a Greek; the relatives of the latter undertook to avenge the insult; the parties came to blows, and several individuals on both sides were killed in the affray.

An account of the affair was laid before Mahomet by one of his ministers. The ferocious Ottoman received the intelligence with joy, and sent a detachment to exterminate the inhabitants of Epibaton. The Turks surprised the harvesters, who, having taken no part in the broil, were working without fear, and massacred forty (June, 1452). This act of hostility was the signal for the last war of the Byzantine empire. At the first alarm the emperor ordered the gates of Constantinople to be closed, and arrested all the Turks who had been attracted to Constantinople either by curiosity or for commercial purposes. Among the number were several pages of the sultan, who were so convinced of the inflexible rigor of their master that they begged as a favor to be beheaded, if they were not permitted to return to the camp before sunset. Constantine gave them their liberty at once, and three days afterwards released the other prisoners. Despairing of averting the storm, he prepared for combat, and the last message of the heir of the Cæsars to Mahomet evinced the firm resignation of a Christian and a soldier. "Since neither the sanctity of your oath, nor the faith of treaties, nor forbearance on our part, can inspire you with sentiments of peace," he said to the sultan, "proceed in your hostile purposes. My confidence is in God alone; if it pleases Him to soften your heart, I shall rejoice in the happy change; if it be His will to deliver Constantinople into your hands, no one can prevent it, and I shall submit without a murmur to His decrees. The gates of the city shall remain closed, and until the Judge of princes decides between us, I will defend my people as long as I have the power to do so."

Far from seeking to justify his conduct, Mahomet immediately declared war. For six months Constantine had foreseen what would inevitably happen, and he had reinforced the garrison of his capital, and collected supplies. About this time the fort on the Bosphorus was completed. As it was placed at the narrowest part of the channel, and it cut off, as it were, the passage from every vessel, the sultan named it *Bohgaz-Kecen* (cut-throat). He confided the command to Firouz-Aga, who had four hundred Janizaries under his orders, directing him to levy a tribute on every vessel which should pass within range of his batteries. In order to enable him to carry out this project, enormous cannons were placed upon the tower of Khalil, which was nearest the sea. On the 28th of August Mahomet left the fort, examined the trenches of Constantinople, and returned to Adrianople on September 1st, 1452.

Before commencing operations, it was necessary to prevent the despots, Demetrius and Thomas, who reigned in Peloponnesus, from sending aid to their brother. To accomplish this, the sultan sent, early in the autumn, an Ottoman army to the peninsula to engage the forces of these princes. It was commanded by Tourakhan, who had grown old in the work of ravaging these countries. His two sons, Ahmed and Omar, accompanied him; they crossed the isthmus of Corinth, entered Arcadia, pushed on as far as Mount Ithone, leaving a mass of ruins behind them, and taking possession of several cities. One division was sent in the direction of Leontari, under the command of Ahmed; but it was surprised by the Greeks, and cut to pieces; the son of Tourakhan was made prisoner, and sent to the despot Demetrius at Sparta.

Whilst his lieutenant was devastating Peloponnesus, Mahomet was making his preparations for the siege of Constantinople. Whilst the work upon the castle of the Bosphorus was in progress, a Hungarian or Dane named Orban, a caster of cannons, who scarcely obtained a subsistence from the Greeks, passed over to the Turks, and offered them the aid of his art. The sultan received him kindly, made him many presents, and assigned him so large a salary that, had the emperor granted him one-fourth of the amount, he would never have left Constantinople. Mahomet was satisfied of his ability at the very first question he put him. "Can you cast me a cannon powerful enough to beat down the walls of Constantinople?" "I know," replied Orban, "the strength and thickness of the walls; but if they were as solid as those of Babylon, I could cast you a cannon which would reduce them to powder. I am certain of all that depends upon my art; but I am not able to determine what will be the range of my piece." "Make me a cannon," said the sultan; "later we can decide upon the range."

According to the orders of Mahomet, a foundry was established at Adrianople, the metal was prepared, and Orban began his work. In three months he furnished a model of enormous size, which was placed on the tower of the new fort commanding the sea. The ship of the Venetian captain Ricci, who wished to pass without lowering his flag, furnished the opportunity of testing its power; the first shot reached the vessel and sunk it instantaneously. Ricci and thirty sailors escaped in a boat, which was driven by the current upon the European shore, and they fell into the hands of the garrison of the castle. The prisoners were conducted in chains to the sultan. He ordered the sailors to be beheaded, the captain to be impaled, and all to be left unburied.

Satisfied with Orban's skill and the success of the trial, Mahomet ordered a colossal cannon double the size of the first. Sixty oxen were required to move this immense mass, and seven hundred men to work it. On his return to Adrianople, the emperor wished to test its power. The cannon was drawn in front of the palace recently constructed; Orban selected the stone and measured the powder. It was loaded with great difficulty. In order to prevent the consequences which might result from the terror of the people, the time when this monstrous piece of artillery would be used was announced by proclamation. At the given signal, a thick black smoke enveloped the whole city; a terrible explosion followed, which was felt or heard to a great distance. The ball buried itself to a considerable depth into the earth a mile distant. This new experiment increased the enthusiasm of the Ottomans, and added to the sad presentiments of the Byzantines.

From that day but one thought occupied the mind of Mahomet—the conquest of Constantinople. He dreamed of it by night, and meditated by day upon the means of making himself master of the city. In the evening, when it was dark, he often walked through the city, accompanied by two confidential friends, in order to listen to the conversation of the people and soldiers. If any one, on meeting him, unfortunately addressed him with the usual salutation: "Long live the sultan!" Mahomet immediately stabbed him to the heart with his own hand. Once he arose about the second watch of the night, and sent his guards to call unexpectedly his first vizier. The message, the hour, the character of the prince, the remembrance of the past and his affection for the Christians, which was so well known that he was called *Gabour-Ortachi*, or foster-brother of the infidels, all alarmed the conscience of Khalil-Pasha. He thought himself lost; he embraced his wife and children, whom he feared he would never see again, provided himself with a cup filled with gold pieces, and hastened to the palace. The vizier found the sultan dressed and seated on the side of his bed. He prostrated himself before him, and, according to the Oriental custom, offered him the gold he had brought. "What are you doing, Lala?" said Mahomet. "When the officers of the empire," replied Khalil, "are called by their masters at extraordinary hours, they should never appear with their hands empty; I present you, not what belongs to me, but what is your own." "I do not need it," answered the sultan, "I would rather heap benefits upon your head. I ask of you only one thing, which is very near my heart: help me to take Constantinople."

At these words the grand vizier shuddered; for he was the secret friend of the Greeks, having been won over by their gifts. Recovering from his surprise, he replied: "The same God who has given you so large a portion of the Roman empire, will not refuse to open to you likewise the gates of the capital. The favors He has been pleased to shower upon you, and your great power, assure me that this city will not escape your grasp. Do not doubt it, my lord; your faithful servants will sacrifice wealth and life to procure the success of our enterprise." "I have tossed all night upon my bed," resumed Mahomet, "I arose, I lay down again, I could not sleep. But I will combat the Romans in such a manner that, confiding in God and his prophet, we shall not fail to take Constantinople." Thus he dismissed his grand vizier, whose anxiety he had quieted by the kindness of his words. Forever tormented by his projects of conquest, the sultan enjoyed no repose. He employed his leisure hours in tracing the plans of the capital of the Greek empire, its walls, its fortifications—in discussing with his generals and engineers the points of attack, the disposition of the different army corps, the situation of the machines and batteries, the places where mines could be sprung or scaling ladders applied. He effected in the day what he had planned in the night.

Whilst Mahomet was menacing the last asylum of Christianity in the East, Constantine, feeling that the last hour of the empire was at hand, implored heaven with fervent prayers and cast to the West an expiring cry of alarm. But his voice was unheeded amid the hostilities of kings and nations, more powerful over men than their common danger. If Europe seemed to view with indifference the storm which was about to burst over Constantinople, and to overthrow the bulwark of Christian society, it was because she was herself experiencing a terrible crisis, and because all her nations were harassed by war.

In the North, Sweden and Norway, which had been temporarily united under the sway of the celebrated Margaret Waldemar, had just been divided into three kingdoms (1448). The effort to reunite these into one caused a century of wars. Therefore the Scandanavian states, surrounded moreover by idolatrous Finns and Laplanders, refused to combat the enemies of the faith before the walls of Byzantium. It would seem that conformity of doctrine and religious ceremonies should have interested

Russia more deeply than the other powers in the misfortunes of tne Greeks. But Russia, still a prey to her Tartar conquerors, could only attend to her own miseries, and above all, desired to regain her independence by shaking off the yoke of the hated foreigner. Though Poland, under the Jagellons, was the dominant power of the North, though she had more than once disputed the possession of Hungary and Bohemia with Austria, and given sovereigns to these two kingdoms, yet there were sources of weakness within her, concealed for the time, but which were soon to cause her downfall, and make her lose the rank to which she had been elevated by the exertion of her kings. Prussia had not yet entered into the family of nations.

England was not disposed to undertake distant expeditions: the weak Henry VI. of the house of Lancaster, heir of the victor of Agincourt, had just lost one of his crowns, and felt that the other was about to fall from his head. Richard of York was preparing to assert the claims of his family. The parliament, shorn of its power under Henry IV. and Henry V., aspired to regain its ancient influence. Thus in England were fomenting those internal dissensions, those vicissitudes of the long struggle between the houses of York and Lancaster, which for a half century were to paralyze her forces. The Scotch excused themselves upon the plea of the distance, and their king, James II., but little interested in the calamities of the East, after a stormy minority, thought only of restoring order and peace to his state, of diminishing the power of the aristocracy and promulgating laws advantageous to the crown.

France, whose nobles had so frequently signalized their courage against the infidels in Africa, Europe and Asia, learned with deep sorrow the triumphs of Islamism. But after the long and terrible war which had arrested her progress and long endangered her independence, she was slowly recovering from its effects, and desired peace to heal her wounds and enjoy the wise government of Charles VII. Like the king of Scotland, the king of France was surrounded by powerful vassals, and he was dealing blows against these feudal nobles, and preferred to banish anarchy from his own kingdom, rather than fight, without profit, the warlike Ottomans.

Spain, divided into several kingdoms, and isolated, as it were, from the rest of Europe, had on her hands an uninterrupted crusade against the Moors of Granada, and she could not spare her forces for a foreign warfare. The emperor could ask aid against the formidable armies of Mahomet II. neither from Switzerland, which had just concluded a long struggle with the dukes of Austria, nor from Italy, which was cut up into small states, divided in their interests and views, jealous of each other, corrupted by luxury, without public morals, and themselves defended by mercenary troops.

The empire, Hungary and Bohemia, which would be unprotected from the sword of the enemy should the Mussulmans triumph over the Greeks, were the only nations upon whom it seemed any reliance for help could be placed. But at this period, the emperor Frederick III., of the house of Austria, was far from possessing the same power as the ancient Cæsars. Under the reign of this prince Germany, distracted by civil wars, which were often repressed but as often renewed, was in no condition to oppose the progress of the ferocious conquerors who threatened Europe with another invasion. Whilst Constantine's ambassadors were traversing the West, imploring aid from every Christian prince, the selfish and heartless Frederic was occupied only with his own affairs and the aggrandizement of his family, and he went to Rome to receive from the pope the imperial crown. The kingdom of Hungary, one of the most powerful nations of Europe in the twelfth century, lost much power and influence, after the prerogatives of the magnates and barons had been increased by a new constitution, to the detriment of the royal authority. The crown, which was now elective, was worn at that time by Ladislaus the Posthumous, under the regency of John Hunniades. This hero, having made peace with the Ottomans, turned his entire attention to the affairs of Hungary and Austria. Ladislaus the Posthumous, also reigned over Bohemia, under the guardianship of Podiebrad. But the unsettled condition both of political and religious affairs in this state prevented her from turning her forces against the Turks. Thus Europe, grown old in dissensions and swayed by diverse interests, was unable to make an effort to save the Byzantine empire, whose long and painful agony she had viewed for years with indifference.

Constantine, who expected to see his capital besieged at the commencement of spring, sent envoys to the islands and provinces inhabited by Christians, to purchase grain and other provisions. Four large vessels sailed for the isle of Chios, whence they were directed to bring corn, wine, oil, pease and barley. Besides these four vessels, another was expected from Morea, and the five were to return to Constantinople at the same time, bearing soldiers and sailors. The inhabitants of these islands were agitated by an uncertainty mingled with fear and hope. Some believed that Mahomet would make himself master of the city; others were persuaded that his enterprise would not be more successful than that of his father and grandfather, all whose efforts were baffled by the energetic defence of the Greeks. Before following the sultan to the siege of the capital of the Byzantine empire, it will not be amiss to give some historical and topographical account of this celebrated city.

Situated in the Eastern extremity of Europe, in the most magnificent position, Constantinople, like Rome, is built on seven hills. It was called Byzantium from the navigator Byzas, its first founder (656 B. C.); then Constantinople, from Constantine, who selected it for his residence and introduced Christianity. In digging the ground and clearing away the rubbish, by order of the emperor, there were found, according to ancient historians, strange to say, old medals stamped with a crescent. Before resuming this symbol under Mahomet II., the city was to subsist a thousand years under the sign of the cross. The degenerate Greeks afterwards called it *Istambol;* this was altered by the Turks into *Islambul*, signifying in their language, "plenitude of Islam." They also bestowed upon it the pompous title of Mother of the World (Oumm-Uddunïa). Queen of two continents and two seas, the vast commercial mart of the East and West, the second Rome, at first a rival of ancient Rome and soon surpassing her elder sister and enriched with her spoils, is placed at the extremity of the two parts of the world, almost enveloped by water and joining the land only by a single point at Thrace. We may represent it to ourselves as an irregular triangle, of which the obtuse angle, projecting towards the shores of Asia, is washed by the waves of the Bosphorus. Towards the south it overlooks the Sea of Marmora, anciently known under the name of Propontis, and the straits of Dardanelles, formerly the Hellespont. From the former of these seas the navigator can follow the steep coast of Thrace, and behold the summit of Olympus crowned with perpetual snow. The narrowest part of the Hellespont is between the ancient cities of Sestos and Abydos. It was here that Xerxes constructed his marvellous bridge of boats to convey his army into Europe.

On the eastern side, Constantinople commands the winding length of the Bosphorus, which, like an immense serpent, forms seven coils, concealing its waves at intervals behind the seven promontories of each of its coasts. If the temples and expiatory altars, which Greek navigators scattered profusely over rocks and shores, were proofs of their fears and ignorance, in our days a vast panorama gives evidence of the life of a great people. This panorama unfolds to our view, dotted with towers, villages and palaces, presenting to the eye, in the incomparable passage of the Bosphorus, elegant kiosks, charming dwellings, and superb edifices, with an admirable chaos of red roofs, old cypress trees, and the white spires of three hundred and forty-four mosques. From the southern outlet of the strait, the view extends to the Euxine Sea. The new forts of Europe and Asia are constructed on both continents. The ancient castles, the work of the Greek emperors, which formerly served as State prisons, and which were called the *Towers of Lethe*, guard the narrowest part of the channel. At its northern extremity, the Bosphorus makes towards the west a turn resembling the horn of a cow, terminating in the most magnificent and safest harbor in the world. This harbor is always filled with vessels from every nation of the globe. Its form and the wealth which naturally flows thither have obtained it the appropriate name of the Golden Horn.

At the period of the siege of Constantinople by Mahomet II., there was a fort at each point of the triangle. The Acropolis, situated upon the promontory, now called the *Seraglio*, was the castle of St. Demetrius. At the extremity of the harbor lay the *Cynegion*, the Haïwan Seraï of the present day, a vast circular enclosure destined for the combats of wild beasts; beyond this was the palace of Blachernes, the favorite residence of the last Greek emperors. At the third angle, that is at the other extremity of the wall on the land side, arose the *Cyclobion* or *Pentapyrgion* (five towers); this fortress afterwards became famous under the name of the Seven Lovers. Between the Acropolis and Pentapyrgion, two basins had been dug; these were beautified by the palaces of the Emperors Theodosius and Julian, by whose orders the work had been completed and which bore their names: they are now filled with sand. The grand imperial palace occupied very nearly the site of the present Seraglio.

Terrified by the extensive preparations of the sultan, the Greeks recalled all the sinister predictions which had long been circulated among them in regard to the destinies of the reigning dynasty, the capital and empire, and even of Christendom.

There were fourteen gates in the city opening on the harbor: two of these, the gate of the Circus and the Golden Gate, through which the triumphal processions usually passed, had been walled up in consequence of an ancient prophecy that through them the conquerors would enter the city. This tradition still exists among the Turks, who believe that the Christians at some future day will regain possession of Islambul, and will re-enter the city of Constantine through the Golden Gate and re-establish the religion of their fathers. Another still more ancient prediction, attributed to a holy man named Morenus, asserted that a people armed with bows and arrows would exterminate the Greeks.

Other reports arising from superstition and fear circulated among the people. Whilst these had the effect of redoubling the ardor of the Mussulmans, they deprived the Greeks of all energy, and seemed, by their fatal influence, to prepare the catastrophe they announced. Now the ruin of the Byzantine empire was read in the oracles attributed to the sibyl of Erythrea; again, Leo the Wise had made discoveries in the convent of St. George predicting its downfall. It was also said that a soothsayer, on being consulted by Michael, the first of the Palæologi, in reference to the destiny of the empire and his successors, had answered with one word, *mamaimi*, which, being composed of seven letters, indicated, according to interpreters, that the sovereignty of the family of the Palæologi would end with the seventh of the name, who would be contemporary with the seventh Ottoman sultan. Finally, John Hunniades, in his flight after the battle of Kossora, had met an old man gifted with the spirit of prophecy. The hero related to him his misfortunes, and testified his sorrow that fortune had abandoned the Greeks and favored the infidels. To console him for his defeat, the old man said: "The Christians will suffer reverses until the Greeks are exterminated. To put an end to their misfortunes, Constantinople must fall into the hands of the Turks."

CHAPTER VIII.

SIEGE AND FALL OF CONSTANTINOPLE—DESTRUCTION OF THE EMPIRE OF THE EAST.

Transportation of the great cannon before the walls of Constantinople—Commencement of the siege—Ambassadors from John Hunniades in the Turkish camp—Forces of the Ottomans and the Greeks—Attack and defence—Victory of the five vessels bearing aid to the Greeks—Council held by Mahomet—He transports his ships across the land—Justinian fails in an attempt to burn the Turkish fleet—Distress of the city—Reply of Mahomet to a message from Constantine—A second attempt of the Christians to burn the bridge and the sultan's fleet—Final message of Mahomet to the Greek emperor—Noble answer of Constantine—Preparations made by the Turks for a general assault—Constantine rouses the courage of the Greeks—The Genoese repair the breaches made in the walls—The sultan makes useless efforts to corrupt Justinian—A second council assembled by Mahomet—Last adieu of the emperor and the Greeks—The general assault—Death of the emperor—Fall of the city—Pillage of Constantinople—Captivity of the Greeks—Departure of the Italian vessels.

EARLY in February, 1453, Mahomet ordered the immense cannon of Orban to be placed before the walls of Constantinople. It was drawn by sixty oxen; two hundred men walked on each side to keep it erect; two hundred and fifty workmen preceded it to level the ground and repair the roads. Two months were required to make a two days' journey. Karadjabeg, who was appointed to superintend the removal, occupied the leisure time afforded by so slow a march in making excursions to the north and south of Constantinople; he even proceeded as far as the shores of the Black Sea, and the Propontis. On the way he subjugated the cities of Mesembria, Anchialos, Byzon and the Castle of

St. Stephen, not far from Constantinople. The garrison of the latter were massacred in punishment of their resistance. Other fortresses surrendered at the first summons and received no injury; but the Turks made a frightful example of those who attempted to defend themselves. Selymbria, however, did not appear dismayed by the consequences, and trusting in the strength of her walls, she determined to repulse courageously the enemy's attack. But all efforts were vain against the conqueror, who extended his ravages to the very gates of Constantinople.

At the commencement of the month of March, Mahomet published throughout the provinces an order commanding all his subjects capable of bearing arms to follow him to the siege of Constantinople. Besides those who were obliged to go, a crowd of volunteers flocked to his standard. Old men and children were eager to take part in the holy war. The sultan commanded the army in person, and on the Friday after Easter, April 6, 1453, he appeared before Constantinople and placed his tent in the rear of the hill which faced the gate called Caligaria. His troops covered the whole plain. The large cannon was drawn up before the gate St. Romain, afterwards called by the name it now bears of Big-Cannon. By the side of this piece were two others of less calibre, intended to prepare the way for the large cannon. Two hours were required to load this piece, and it could be fired only eight times in the day; the first shot before dawn was the signal for the commencement of the attack.

John Hunniades, as mentioned above, had concluded with Mahomet a truce of three years. He now sent an envoy to the Ottoman camp to represent to the sultan that he had resigned the administration of affairs into the hands of Ladislaus, his master; being, therefore, no longer able to fulfill the conditions of the treaty, he returned the Turkish copy which he had held, and asked in exchange the Hungarian copy in the possession of Mahomet, who would then be at liberty to make such arrangements as might please him with the King of Hungary. The prophecy of which we spoke above had influenced the regent to take this step; and for his part, the ambassador considered it a duty to secure the repose and safety of Christendom by hastening the fall of Constantinople, and thus accomplishing the prediction of the old man. One day, being present when the great cannon was fired, he ridiculed the engineer who directed the aim, and instructed him how to use the piece advantageously. He taught him in making a breach not to aim always at the same spot, but to fire alternately a certain distance to the right and to the left, and then in the centre, so as to break down the wall already weakened by the previous shot. The Turks followed his advice, and success soon crowned their efforts. Thus it was a Hungarian artificer who cast the cannon, and a Hungarian ambassador who taught the Turks the method of using it.

Besides Orban's enormous piece, and the two smaller ones on each side of it, the Turks arranged a long line of less powerful batteries against the walls, and fourteen ballista played incessantly upon the most accessible parts. The archers poured upon the besieged a shower of arrows; the miners from the mountains of Novoberda pushed their work up to the very trench of the city. Mahomet ordered to be constructed four towers mounted upon wheels, and a gigantic machine named by the Greeks *Epepolia* (that which takes cities). It was put in motion by cylinders; a triple covering of ox-hides protected this movable magazine, carrying ammunition and materials to fill up the trench. The upper story consisted of turrets and parapets, which permitted the men within to shoot through openings without being themselves exposed to danger. There were three doors in the lower part, by which the soldiers could make sorties, and the workmen could enter and retire. A stairway gave access to the platform on the top of the machine; from this could be lowered a sort of drawbridge, which being fastened to the rampart of the enemy, rendered a close combat easy.

Ducas estimates the Turkish army under the walls of Constantinople at two hundred thousand men; Leonard of Chios, at three hundred thousand. The latter is an exaggergated account, and we adopt that of of Phranza, who places the numbers at two hundred and fifty-eight thousand men. Thus the Ottomans had a force twenty times as large as that of the besieged; and moreover the ardor of the intrepid fanatics, who were enticed by the sound of the sacred trumpet to the standard of Mahomet, was superior, beyond comparison, to the valor the Greeks could display in their defence.

Constantinople contained more than a hundred thousand inhabitants; the greater part were workmen, priests, women, and men devoid of courage, upon whom no reliance could be placed. According to an estimate made by the order of the emperor during the siege, Phranza attests that the number of citizens, including the monks, willing to bear arms, did not exceed four thousand nine hundred and seventy-three. To these must be added a body of foreign troops two thousand strong, and about five hundred Genoese under the orders of John Longus, of the noble family of Justiniani, sent on two galleys to the aid of the agonizing empire. Constantine was overpowered with gratitude towards these auxiliaries, and he loaded them with presents. He appointed Longus captain of a body of troops, and granted him the sovereignty of the island of Lemnos, in case Mahomet II. should be forced to abandon the siege. Not only the Greeks cherished this hope, but even the Genoese, masters of Galata, were likewise deceived. They had, it is true, sent ambassadors to the sultan before his departure from Adrianople, assuring him of the fidelity of their friendship, and renewing their former alliance with him. Mahomet promised them to adhere to the letter of the written treaties, and maintain the present condition of peace and friendship, provided they observed a strict neutrality. But the Genoese, distrusting the sincerity of his words, furnished all possible aid to the inhabitants of Constantinople. Informed of the deception, the sultan determined to take his revenge at some future time. "I will let the serpent sleep," he said, "until I have killed the dragon, and then with one blow I will crush his head."

As to the maritime force of the Greeks, it consisted of three large Venetian merchantmen, three Genoese vessels, one French, and one Spanish ship, two from Cydon, and four from Candia. Thus a capital of fourteen miles in circumference was defended against the whole forces of the Ottoman empire only by a garrison of seven or eight thousand soldiers and a navy of fourteen sail. The besiegers could draw resources both from Europe and Asia; the Greeks, enclosed within their walls, were cut off from all assistance.

They were equally inferior to the Ottomans in artillery. A piece of the caliber of Orban's would have been useless to them, for the smallest cannon which they possessed were too heavy for the walls, and weakened them at every discharge by the concussion, so that such arms did more injury to the Greeks than to their enemies. Nevertheless, when one of their large cannon burst, they accused the artificer of having been bribed by Mahomet, and in their fury they were about to put him to death; but not having sufficient proof, they restored him to liberty. At the commencement of the siege, the soldiers descended into the trench or rallied into the open field. But what advantage could one Christian obtain over twenty Mussulmans? Their disproportionate numbers obliged them to limit their attacks to hurling weapons from the ramparts.

We must admit that amid the pusillanimity evinced by the Greek nation in this pressing danger, Constantine displayed the talents and courage of a hero. The noble band of volunteers who had ranged themselves under his standard were animated by the love of their country, and the foreign auxiliaries rivalled them in zeal to maintain worthily the honor of the western chivalry: in a word, we might say that the energy of the victors of Marathon and Salamis was infused into the souls of the generous defenders of Greece. From the midst of the clouds of smoke, the noise and fire of the cannons, they rained on the assailants a shower of javelins and arrows. At the same time they hurled from each of their small arms five or ten leaden balls about the size of a nut, with such force that they pierced shields, breast-plates, and passed through the bodies of several men.

But the Turks, as obstinate in their attack as the Greeks in their defence, soon approached the walls, protected in trenches or by heaps of ruins. Reaching, on one occasion, the sides of the trench, they undertook to fill up the immense opening made by their artillery, and to form a path by which they could make an assault. They heaped up a quantity of bundles of wood, casks and trunks of trees. The activity of the workmen was prodigious, but those who were near the edge, or whose strength was not equal to the task, fell in, and were buried under the mass of wood and other materials thrown upon them. The besieged redoubled their efforts to render fruitless the work of their enemies, and after long and sanguinary contests during the day, they employed the night in destroying the work which the Turks had succeeded in accomplishing. They repaired the breaches with wood and casks filled with stones and earth, while the workmen drove the enemy from the mines they had dug, or arrested their progress by countermines.

John Grant, a worthy rival of the Hungarian auxiliary of the Turks, taught the Greeks a better method of hurling the inextinguishable Greek fire. By means of these liquid flames, they reduced to ashes the large machine with its triple covering of leather, which during the night had demolished the tower of St. Romain. After an obstinate combat, to which the darkness of night alone put an end, the Turks had been repulsed. They flattered themselves that at daybreak they would renew the attack with greater success. But the emperor and the Genoese Justiniani took advantage of the time which the enemy gave to repose and hope. Notwithstanding the fatigues of the preceding day, they passed the night on the walls, surrounded by engineers and workmen, in order to press forward the work upon which depended the safety of Constantinople. At the dawn of day the impatient Mahomet called the soldiers to arms. What was his grief and astonishment at the sight of the trench cleared out and his machine destroyed! He could not, however, forbear paying a just tribute to the defense of the Greeks, and he swore by thirty-seven thousand prophets that he could not have believed the infidels able to accomplish so great a task in a single night.

As soon as Constantine feared his capital would be besieged, he sent, as we have said, to solicit aid from the islands of the Archipelago, Morea and Sicily. Five vessels, laden with grain, barley, oil and vegetables, and carrying soldiers and sailors, had been unable to leave Chios during the whole month of March. One bore the imperial flag; the other four belonged to the Genoese. They took advantage of the first wind from the south to set sail. They crossed the Hellespont and Propontis without accident, and appeared opposite Constantinople. But the Turkish squadron, placed at the entrance of the Bosphorus, extended from one shore to the other in the form of a crescent, for the purpose of preventing the entrance of Christian vessels into the harbor. The sky was serene, and the sea calm. The five vessels advanced with shouts of joy against the hostile fleet. The walls of the city, the camp, the coasts of Europe and Asia, were covered with spectators, anxiously awaiting the arrival of this important aid. Mahomet himself approached the shore to contemplate the preparations for this naval combat, in which the numerical superiority of his vessels seemed to promise him a certain victory. But the crews of the eighteen galleys which occupied the head of his squadron were formed of inexperienced soldiers. The rest consisted of open boats, heavily built, overcrowded with men, and destitute of artillery. Skilful pilots directed the movements of the five vessels of the Christians, which were filled with veterans from Italy and Greece, long accustomed to the labors and dangers of navigation. They endeavored to sink or break to pieces the feeble boats which barred their passage. From their ships, whose cannons swept the waves, fell a shower of arrows, a rain of stones and Greek fire, on the vessels of the enemy which ventured the attempt to board them.

Flectanella, the captain of the imperial vessel, fought in the first ranks like a lion, and performed prodigies of valor. His worthy rivals in glory,

Cataneo, Novarra, and Balameri, commanders of the Genoese squadron, equalled him in courage and energy; by their exertions they saved from destruction the ship of Flectanella, which was in danger of being overpowered by numbers. Several of the Turkish galleys ran into each other and were destroyed; two caught fire. Repulsed in two attacks, the enemy experienced a considerable loss. At the sight of his vessels devoured by the flames, and of the defeat of his men, the Sultan could not restrain the transports of his anger. Forgetting the distance, the element which he braves, and his own dignity, foaming with rage, he makes useless efforts to force his charger into the sea and to snatch the victory from the grasp of the Greeks. The officers surrounding him endeavor likewise to join the fleet. His violent reproaches, his menaces, the fear of his chastisements, and the clamors of the soldiers from the camp, determine the commanders of the Turkish fleet to make a third attack. It was still more fatal than the former two; according to Phranza, they lost more than twelve thousand men. Favored by a wind which blew at the time, the squadron of the Christians advanced triumphantly along the Bosphorus, hailed by the joyous acclamations of the soldiers, sailors, and inhabitants of the besieged city, whilst the Turkish fleet fled in disorder. It entered the harbor under full sail, which was immediately closed by dropping the iron chain extending from a gate of Galata to one in Constantinople.

Mahomet avenged himself for this humiliation upon his admiral, Baltaoghli, a renegade descended from the Princes of Bulgaria, whose fine military qualities were obscured by his avarice. Furious against this commander, to whose cowardice he ascribed the defeat, he ordered him to be executed, but consented to grant him his life at the urgent entreaties of the Janizaries; without any consideration, however, for the rank and services of the unfortunate Baltaoghli, he wished to wreak his vengeance on him with his own hands. Four slaves were ordered to extend the admiral on the ground, and the sultan inflicted upon him one hundred blows with the *topouz* (a kind of club, the emblem of authority). After this ignominious punishment, an azab, not, however, by Mahomet's direction, threw a large stone in his face, which made a deep wound in his cheek and put out an eye. This disaster of the first admiral of the Ottoman empire gave rise to the belief among the Turks that God intended for them the sovereignty by land, but left to the infidels the superiority on the sea.

The aid thus received by the besieged, in so unexpected a manner and in spite of formidable obstacles, raised the hopes of the Greeks, whose obstinate and surprising resistance was beginning, according to their historians, to wear out the perseverance of the sultan. The grand vizier Khalil, won over by the court of Byzantium, with which he had kept up a secret correspondence, and perhaps really desiring the preservation of Constantinople, considered the present a favorable opportunity to induce his master to make peace. But his views were opposed by the second vizier, Saganos Pasha, brother-in-law and favorite of Mahomet, by the mollah Mahomet Hourani, and the cheik Ak-Chems-Uddin, who like

Bokhari, but more successfully, aroused the enthusiasm of the people by his predictions. In a divan held after the repulse of the fleet, the continuation of the siege was resolved upon, notwithstanding the efforts of Khalil, who represented to the sultan that more considerable reinforcements could be sent to the enemy, and that they were uselessly prolonging the combat.

Mahomet saw that he must abandon the project of becoming master of the city, unless an attack by sea could be made simultaneously with an advance of his troops by land. But when he asked his counsellors what means could be employed to break the heavy chain which closed the harbor, in which now lay eight large vessels and twenty smaller ones, besides galleys and boats, they were silent. Then the sultan solved the difficulty by a bold resolution, that of transporting his fleet by land from the shore of the Bosphorus to the remote extremity of the harbor. This laborious operation was successfully and skilfully executed. By Mahomet's order a large platform was constructed and thickly coated with grease. Seventy boats of different sizes were lifted upon rollers and then pushed upon the slippery platform. Two pilots were stationed at the prow and helm of each vessel; the sails were unfurled, the trumpets sounded, drums beat, and shouts and songs relieved the fatigue of the workmen. In the space of one night, the fleet ascended the hill, traversed the plain, and the following morning was moored in the gulf of the Golden Horn. The rising sun discovered to the stupefied inhabitants the vessels of their indefatigable enemy opposite their walls, with a communication open to the sea. In the first moment of consternation, they wished to surrender. The intrepid emperor endeavored to reanimate their courage, and prepared to defend the capital to the last extremity.

Notwithstanding the terror of the Greeks, Justiniani failed not to combat valiantly with his soldiers. A few Genoese, whilst expressing much affection for the Greeks, proved false to both parties. They repaired to the Turkish camp, sold them provisions, oil for greasing their large cannon, and other necessary articles. When night enabled them to return secretly to Constantinople, they joined again the defenders of the city and aided them to repel the assailants. The Venetians displayed uncommon valor, and the grand-duke exhibited the greatest vigilance. He daily visited all the posts of the capital, to see if the soldiers were upon duty and to animate their courage.

Justiniani, having determined to burn the Turkish fleet, prepared a galley for this purpose, manned it with one hundred and fifty young men, the flower of the Italian troops, and collected the necessary machines and fire-works. But the Genoese of Galata, having discovered his intention, betrayed it to the besiegers, who were, consequently, on their guard. When the vessel of the brave Justiniani approached the enemy's squadron about midnight, the Turks fired upon him, and his vessel sank with the warriors on board. The Genoese chief escaped with difficulty, but the greater part of the crew perished in the sea. The cry of distress of the unfortunate companions of Justiniani was answered on the part of the Turks by a shout of victory so loud that Ducas compared the noise to the sound of an earthquake. The victors wished the following morning to try a second time the efficacy of their artillery. They pointed one of their guns, not at a Greek vessel, but at a Genoese boat laden with rich merchandise, which was anchored before Galata: it was shivered to pieces. The Genoese deputies complained bitterly of such a return for the aid afforded by them, and without which the fleet could not have been transported across the land. The viziers apologized by saying that they thought the vessel belonged to the enemy, and that an indemnity for the loss would be granted at the conclusion of the war. The deputies were appeased by these words, not suspecting that they themselves would soon be involved in the common ruin.

The sultan ordered all the young men who had been made prisoners during the night to be conducted before the walls of the city, and massacred in sight of the Greeks. This terrible revenge increased the consternation of the Greeks, whose distress words are inadequate to express. At the end of forty days, the small garrison was exhausted by a two-fold attack; the fortifications, which for nearly two centuries had withstood the successive efforts of the Persians, the Avarians and Arabians, fell under the cannons of the Ottomans. Several breaches had been already made, and four towers near the gate of St. Romain were a mass of ruins. Constantine, destitute of money to pay his enfeebled troops, who were inclined to revolt, was obliged to despoil the churches, promising to return fourfold the value of what he took. At last, misfortune broke the pride of the Greek monarch, and he sent a messenger to propose peace to the sultan, asking him to impose a tribute and withdraw. "It is impossible for me to abandon the siege," replied Mahomet, "I will take the city or it shall take me, alive or dead. If you wish in good faith to leave it, I will give you Morea, I will cede other provinces to your brethren, and we shall remain friends. But if I take it by force of arms, I will strike all the nobles and officials with the sword; I will permit the soldiers to make the people prisoners, and pillage the houses; for my own share of the spoils, I shall be satisfied with the possession of the city and its edifices." A sentiment of honor and the fear of universal blame forbade Palæologus to surrender Constantinople to the infidels.

Encouraged by his recent success and determined not to let the prey escape his grasp, the sultan, now master of the harbor, constructed at the narrowest point a bridge, or rather a mole, fifty cubits wide and a hundred long, formed of casks connected by iron clamps and surmounted by planks firmly fastened. Five soldiers abreast could pass on this mole, upon which was placed one of the large cannons, whilst the galleys and the troops with scaling ladders approached the most accessible part of the wall. The Christians, having in vain endeavored to destroy the works before their completion, conceived the idea of burning the bridge and the vessels. This difficult enterprise was confided to the Venetian James Kok. He selected three small boats, on which forty of the most courageous young sailors embarked, supplied with Greek fire and other combustible materials. They set out in a dark night, leaving on the bridge two sailors with directions to fire it as soon as they saw the flames from the Turkish vessels. But the vigilance of the enemy prevented the execution of this bold project; enormous masses of stone hurled upon their light boats crushed them. Only one galley was burned, and the fire upon the bridge was soon extinguished. The mariners of the small boats fell into the hands of the Turks, and were inhumanly massacred the next day in sight of the besieged.

The failure of this enterprise provoked contentions between the Venetians and the Genoese auxiliaries under the command of Justiniani. The latter threw the blame upon the inexperience of James Kok, and the indignant Venetians warmly defended their compatriot; the emperor was obliged to interpose, to prevent a bloody contest. Besides, the spirit of discord increased daily, and diminished the strength of the Christians. Mahomet now ordered batteries to be placed upon the hill of St. Theodore, situated above Galata, with orders to fire indiscriminately upon all vessels, whether Greek or Genoese. The Genoese, in alarm, sent deputies to supplicate the sultan to spare their merchant vessels. Mahomet replied that he only treated in this manner pirates who afforded aid to the besieged. Fearing to expose their boats, the inhabitants placed them in a position to be sheltered by the houses.

For seven weeks the siege had continued without relaxation by land, and now the city was invested by sea. In preceding sieges, it had been seriously menaced only at one point. But now the Turks occupied the trench, which was nearly filled with the ruins of the towers and fortifications; their artillery had made a large breach in the St. Romain gate, and their vessels were approaching the most accessible point. When Mahomet considered his arrangements so far perfected as to enable him to possess himself of Constantinople, he sent a final message to the emperor by his son-in-law, Esfendiar-Oghlou, either to fulfil his duty as a Mussulman of offering to the *gabours* the alternative of embracing the religion of the prophet and submitting to pay tribute, or of resigning themselves to death, or to assure himself by an eye-witness if the city were able to prolong the resistance. The message was couched in the following terms: "All things are ready for an attack, and I am about to execute what I decided upon long ago. The result is in the hands of God. What will you do? Will you depart from your capital with the nobles of your empire, taking with them all their wealth, the inhabitants to remain secure from ill treatment either from your people or mine? Should you determine to defend yourselves to the last extremity, you shall be deprived of property and life, the people shall be enslaved and dispersed over the whole earth."

Efendiar-Oghlou, being admitted to the presence of the emperor, who was surrounded by his court, advised him to avoid the wrath of the sultan, and by a timely submission spare his people the miseries of slavery. A council of war was held, and the decision was such as honor demanded. Constantine replied nobly to the Turkish ambassador:

"If you will live at peace with us, as your ancestors lived with our ancestors, we shall return humble thanks to Almighty God. Your ancestors honored ours as their fathers. They regarded Constantinople as their country; here they found an asylum under every misfortune. Not one of all those who ventured to attack the capital of the Roman empire lived long. Be satisfied with retaining undisturbed the provinces and cities of which you have unjustly deprived us. Impose upon us as heavy a tribute as you choose, and then withdraw your forces. The fortune of war is uncertain, and perhaps at the very time that you flatter yourself with having secured the conquest of our city, you may experience a reverse. As to a surrender of the city, we do not en-entertain the thought. We are all determined to to die in its defence."

Mahomet employed three days after the reception of this answer in making his preparations. On the 24th of May he publicly appointed the 29th as the day for a simultaneous attack by sea and land. He assembled the chief officers of the army, and relying on the effect of temporal recompense, he solemnly promised the soldiery the pillage of the city. "It belongs to me," he said to them, "as well as the buildings; but I renounce in your favor the captives, the booty, and all its wealth." A shout of joy from the army welcomed this announcement of the sultan. The chiefs of the Janizaries promised him the victory in the name of the soldiers, and begged him to restore to liberty their unfortunate comrades, who had been kept in prison since the disastrous naval combat... Mahomet complied with their request, and the whole army abandoned itself to transports of joy. To excite their enthusiasm still more, the sultan announced that *timars*, and even *sandjaks*, should be the recompense of those who should first mount the ramparts. At the same time he proclaimed that fugitives and deserters should experience no mercy.

The dervishes, whose zeal Mahomet had inflamed by his promises, traversed the camp, in order to inspire the soldiers with the desire of martyrdom. They conjured the Mussulmans in the name of the prophet to plant the standard of Islamism on the battlements of the city of the infidels. Their impetuous exhortations excited among the Turks an eager desire for the combat. The camp resounded with songs and the oft-repeated acclamation: "God is God, and Mahomet is His prophet! God is one, and there is none like to Him!" When darkness enveloped the earth, the trumpets sounded the signal for a general illumination of the camp and fleet. Immediately there sprung up waves of light from the tents, from the shores of the Bosphorus, from the heights above Galata, from the extremity of the harbor, and along the whole line of fortifications. The blaze of the fire-works was reflected from Scutari and the Asiatic shore. At the sight of the semicircle of light surrounding them, hope, for a moment, raised the drooping spirits of the besieged. They thought that an immense conflagration was consuming the tents and the fleet of the Turks; but the dances and joyous shouts soon dispelled the illusion, and they felt that this was but a prelude to the triumph of the barbarians. It would be impossible to describe the sad spectacle presented by the city of Constantine. Despair filled all hearts; naught was heard but lamentations, and as a wail arose the plaintive cry: "Kyrie, eleison! Kyrie, eleison! Turn away Thy anger from us, O Lord, and deliver us not into the hands of our enemies!"

In this trying moment, the emperor visited in person every post; he assembled the noblest among the Greeks and the bravest of the auxiliaries, to prepare them for the general assault they were about to sustain, and to exhort them to do their duty. He neglected no means to excite the courage of his subjects. During the seven weeks of siege they had already endured, they had flattered themselves with the hope that the enemy would not venture to scale the walls. In consequence of this, many of the inhabitants had left the ramparts and returned to their homes. The Turks took advantage of the opportunity thus presented, and by means of enormous hooks, removed the gabions which the besieged used to fill up the breaches made by the enemy. The men who had deserted their posts gave as a reason to Constantine, who overwhelmed them with reproaches, that their wives and children had no food. The emperor ordered provisions to be distributed to the men and throughout the houses along the line of defence.

In the meantime, Justiniani had worked without relaxation in repairing the breaches made by the Turks in the wall near the gate of St. Romain. By means of bundles of sticks, the Genoese had raised a new fortification, behind which they dug a deep trench. Seeing the labors and efforts of the brave

Italians, the sultan exclaimed: "What would I not give to secure the services of such a man!" He made him secret offers and endeavored to win him by presents; but he found him as inaccessible to his gold as to his sword. Justiniani exhausted himself in useless efforts to repair the fortifications, for they had not been put in a condition suitable for defence whilst time and money were at the command of the Greeks. The Monks, Manuel Giagari and Neophytus of Rhodes, to whose care the repairs had been committed previous to the siege by the Turks, had buried the money furnished them for the purpose; and when the city was pillaged, seventy thousand gold pieces which they had secreted were found.

Deplorable as was the state of the city, the Greeks prepared to defend it. At the gate St. Romain, against which the fiercest attack was directed, were stationed the choicest Genoese troops, with Justiniani at their head; there also were the emperor and Don Francis of Toledo. The defence of ten other posts was assigned to efficient officers, of known valor—Genoese, Venetians, Spanish, Germans and Russians. The Greeks had command of only two. Some historians compute the whole available force of the garrison, including the monks who took up arms, at nine thousand men at most.

Again the hopes of the besieged were aroused by a report circulated through the Ottoman camp that an army of Hungarians and Italians were marching to the relief of Constantinople. The Mussulmans became so terror-stricken that, notwithstanding the enthusiasm of the eve and their numerical superiority, they remained inactive for two days. But their courage was revived on the third day by the sight of a meteor which flashed across the heavens from the northwest over the city, as they regarded this phenomenon as a sign of the divine protection. Mahomet, who had wavered in his purpose of making an assault, assembled his council a second time. The pacific measures urged by Khalil were opposed by his former adversaries. In his anger the grand vizier ventured to give secret information to the Greeks, urging them to make a vigorous resistance, as in war victory was always uncertain. This passed on the evening of the 27th of May.

On the following morning, Mahomet ranged his army in two grand columns for the attack by land. A formidable fleet of eighty galleys blockaded the city on the side of the sea. The Turkish forces opposite the Golden Gate numbered one hundred thousand men. To the left of the camp fifty thousand were drawn up in echelons. A reserve of a hundred thousand were ready to support the above corps if necessity should require it. About sunset an extraordinary excitement was observed in the Turkish camp; the clash of arms and the flourish of trumpets mingled with cries of *La Ilah illalah!* The sultan, surrounded by the high officials of the Ottoman empire, reviewed his troops, harangued the generals, and excited their ardor by the most tempting promises.

On his side, the emperor endeavored to reanimate in the hearts of the Greeks and the auxiliaries the hope he no longer cherished. His address to the troops, preserved by the historian Phranza, may be considered the funeral oration of the Byzantine empire. The example of their prince, the misfortunes of the beleaguered city, roused his warriors to the courage of despair. They wept, they embraced each other; they devoted themselves to death. Every officer was at his post during the night, and kept guard on the ramparts. Constantine, accompanied by the members of his household, repaired to the church of St. Sophia. They prayed, they received the Holy Communion amid the sobs of the crowd who thronged the edifice. Returning to the palace, the emperor allowed himself a few moments of repose; he begged pardon of the weeping multitude for any offence of which he might have been guilty in their regard. Having fulfilled his religious duties, the emperor devoted his entire attention to the safety of the capital. He mounted his horse, and, followed by his faithful companions, visited every post in the city to encourage the soldiers to do their duty. The fall of the last of the Constantines, says Gibbon, is more glorious than the prosperity of the Cæsars of Byzantium. At early dawn the emperor was at the gate St. Romain, determined to conquer or to die.

At sunrise, on the 29th of May, 1453, the Turks commenced the assault, without firing, as usual, their great cannon, and instantaneously it extended throughout the whole line, both by land and sea. In order to fatigue the Greeks and spare his best troops, Mahomet had composed the van of volunteers who fought without order or discipline, and of those who had joined his standard from the hope of plunder. The artillery of the army corps, of the galleys and of the bridge, battered Constantinople simultaneously. An invincible courage was displayed on both sides, and the Turkish loss was considerable. The whole city appeared surrounded by a close and unbroken line of hostile troops. Cries of terror and screams of pain mingled with the noise of drums, trumpets, cymbals and the discharge of artillery. At the end of two hours the Turks had gained no perceptible advantage. The sultan's officers of justice were placed behind the assailants, and urged them on by blows of iron rods. Mahomet, on horseback and armed with an iron club, employed, by turns, promises and threats, and directed and animated the host of warriors. To these immense efforts of the Ottomans, the Greeks opposed a heroic valor. A shower of arrows and stones fell upon those who were mounting to the assault; the terrible Greek fire flowed down the walls into the sea, set fire to the ships, and spread in a sheet of flame over the water. Thick clouds of smoke enveloped the camp, the city, the besiegers and besieged. The trench was filled with the bodies of the slain, as the sultan hoped, and yet they had not reached the ramparts. Hurled from the scaling-ladders or crushed by stones, the men fell upon their vessels' decks or into the harbor.

Seconded nobly by Theophilus Palæologus and Demetrius Cantacuzenus, the emperor passed from post to post, encouraged his troops by word and example, and successfully repulsed the assailants. Victory seemed almost in the grasp of Constantine and his brave companions; deaf to the menaces of Mahomet, the Turks were giving way, when a ball or arrow pierced the hand of Justiniani. This man, whom Ducas calls an incomparable general, a formidable giant, could not bear the sight of his own blood and the extreme pain caused by the wound. "Hold your ground," he said to the emperor, "whilst I retire to my vessel to have my wound dressed; I will return immediately." "Your wound is not serious," exclaimed the emperor; "the danger is imminent, your presence is necessary; besides, how will you be able to leave the city?" "I shall take the road," replied the Genoese, "which God Himself has opened for the Turks." Saying these words, he passed through a breach in the interior wall and fled to Galata, forever dishonoring by this cowardly act a life of glory. Justiniani did not long survive his shame, and his last moments were imbittered by the remorse of his own conscience and the contempt of all good men. The Genoese imitated the example of their chief and fled from the city, with the greater part of the Latin auxiliaries. Seeing them depart Constantine exclaimed: "Let us who remain, be faithful and do our duty."

Up to this time, the valor of the besieged had compensated for the breaches made in the double walls, broken in every direction by the artillery of the enemy, which played upon them incessantly; but the assailants outnumbered the besieged by fifty to one, and the retreat of Justiniani and the Genoese dismayed the remaining troops. Saganos-Pasha, who noticed some disorder in their ranks, urged his Janizaries to renewed exertion. One of them, Hassan d'Ouloubad, of gigantic size and immense strength, was the first to win the recompense promised by the sultan. With a cimeter in his right hand and holding in his left a shield above his head, he sprang upon the wall, followed by thirty companions, his rivals in courage; they were received with showers of arrows and stones; eighteen Janizaries were precipitated from the wall at the same time. But having reached the summit, Hassan and his twelve companions defend themselves; but he is himself thrown from the wall, and his body is soon covered with arrows and stones.

Whilst the Greeks were thus valiantly defending the St. Romain gate, against which the principal attack was directed, the Turks had already entered the city on another side. The eve of the 29th, the gate Cercoporta, by the order of the emperor, who wished to surprise Mahomet's camp by an unexpected sortie, had been opened, but by a fatal carelessness it was not closed. Fifty Turks forced this passage, mounted the walls, and poured with irresistible impetuosity upon the combatants. At that moment a cry arose from the harbor that the city was in the hands of the enemy; this disordered the ranks of those who were still resisting. Constantine, seeing the Greeks give way and falling back upon St. Sophia, abandoned the ground to the invaders, and rushed with a few brave men towards the largest breach, hoping to rally them by his example. He fought like a lion with indomitable courage, overthrew all who crossed his path, was covered with his own blood and that of the infidels, and piled the dead in heaps around him. By his side, John of Dalmatia vainly multiplied his prodigies of valor; Francis of Toledo, whose great heart knows not fear, surpasses Achilles, and pounces like an eagle upon his prey. Theophilus Palæologus exclaims: "I would rather die than live," and disappearing amid the enemy, finds a glorious death. Constantine is left alone: "What!" he says sorrowfully, "is there not one Christian who will deliver me from these miseries?" As he spoke, he fell under the sabre strokes of two Ottomans, one of whom struck him in the face, the other in the back; and the seventh of the line of the Palæologi, Constantine Dragoses, the last of the Greek emperors, lay amid the numerous victims of this fatal day.

With the death of the emperor, resistance ceased; the rout was general, and the Turks rushed in through Caligaria gate, after having crossed the heap of dead bodies which filled the trenches. Supposing that they had still to combat a garrison of fifty thousand men, and that they would meet the same opposition in every section of the city, they massacred all the soldiers who were endeavoring to escape. In the first heat of the pursuit, two thousand victims were thus immolated; at last they became aware of the real weakness of the Greeks, and put an end to the carnage, because it was more advantageous to the victors to secure prisoners, who were a bait to their avarice. The inhabitants, overpowered by terror, ran in crowds towards the harbor, of which the enemy did not yet hold possession. The fifty Turks who had first obtained entrance had been repulsed, and many fugitives made good their escape to the Greek and Genoese vessels. The guards, seeing the numbers who were hastening to the harbor rapidly increasing, closed the gates and threw the keys into the sea.

Such was the size of Constantinople, that for a time many of the inhabitants were ignorant of the sad fate which awaited them. When the report was circulated that the Turks had entered the city, some refused to believe it; but a few moments sufficed to destroy their false security. As soon as the public misfortune was known as a certainty, the houses and convents were deserted; the trembling inhabitants collected in the streets and in the squares like bands of timid animals; then, upon hearing that the Turks were approaching, they took refuge in the church of St. Sophia, towards which rushed also the crowd which had been driven back from the harbor. In less than an hour the sanctuary, the nave, the galleries, were filled with old men, women, and children, who barred the doors.

The Turks arrived, broke open the doors, and the work of destruction commenced. Nothing arrested them; neither the groans of fathers, nor the tears of women, nor the weakness of old men, nor the cries of children, nor the supplications of the wounded. In the course of an hour all the men were bound with ropes, the women with their veils and cinctures. The streets were filled with these unhappy captives, led by the conquerors in long files like animals destined for slaughter. If any attempted to resist, they were compelled by blows to hasten their steps; for the invaders were eager to secure additional booty. The same scenes of rapine and desolation were repeated in every convent and church, in every palace and dwelling of this once powerful city. The number reduced to slavery during the sack, which lasted three days, is estimated to have been sixty thousand; the captives were exchanged or sold, according to the caprice or interest of their masters, and dispersed in different provinces of the Ottoman empire.

Driven by despair at the sight of the enemy entering Constantinople, the historian Phranza, chief secretary of the emperor, precipitated himself into the midst of the Turks, but, although, he did not witness the death of his master, he did not find the death he sought for himself; he fell with his family into the hands of the victors. After four months of slavery, he succeeded in recovering his liberty, and the following year he went to Adrianople and redeemed his wife, who belonged to the chief of cavalry; his son and daughter were dead. Cardinal Isadore, to whom had been intrusted the defence of the line extending from the gate of the Cynegion to the church of St. Demetrius, was among the prisoners. It is said that, seeing the city must fall, he dressed himself as a common citizen, was sold as a captive of no value, and after having incurred many dangers, he made his escape to Rome.

The church of St. Sophia, the wonder of the world, the temple elevated to the honor of God, was not spared. The statues, master-pieces of sculpture, were broken to pieces, the gold and silver vessels were removed or destroyed, and horses were fed at the altar.

The Greeks still held possession of the ramparts facing the harbor, which had not yet been attacked, and they remained at their posts until the invaders fell upon them from the rear. At the same time, another portion of the Ottoman army scaled the walls not far from the gate of Petra. Then the fleet, which still held possession of the chain and the entrance of the exterior harbor, and which had signalized its valor by its resistance to the Turks, took advantage of the moment when the Turkish crew were engaged in the work of pillage to make their escape. Resistance now became impossible, and the defenders of the ramparts only thought of their own safety. All the gates were broken open, and the enemy poured in with impetuosity. As the grand duke Lucas Notaras saw the Turks approaching the post committed to his charge, he retreated towards his palace, followed by a small number of his companions. Some fell into the hands of the Turks before reaching their dwellings; others found in their homes neither wife nor children, nor goods. They were made captive, and were not permitted to mourn the loss they had sustained. Old men, incapable from their infirmities or age of marching with the rest, were massacred without mercy, and children were cast into the streets and public squares. Lucas Notaras was arrested as he gained his dwelling; Orklan, grandson of Soliman, who had been brought forward by the Greeks as an aspirant to the throne in opposition to Mahomet, precipitated himself from the top of a tower to escape falling into the hands of the sultan, whose cruelty he dreaded.

A sad scene was witnessed when the Italian vessels prepared to leave Constantinople. The shore was thronged with men, women, children and religious, who with tears and entreaties implored the sailors to take them on board. But it was decreed that they should drink the bitter chalice to the dregs. The vessels did not suffice to convey the great numbers begging to be received: the Venetians and Genoese selected their own countrymen, and abandoned the rest to their fate. It would be impossible to describe the rage of Mahomet at the sight of the boats thus eluding his grasp. The inhabitants of Galata escaped, carrying with them such precious articles as they could collect together. Saganos-Pasha, Mahomet's favorite minister, strove to arrest their flight and swore to them by the head of the sultan that no injury should be done them. "Do not depart," he cried to them from the shore, "fear nothing. You are the friends of the sultan; your city shall be inviolate; no hostile act shall be committed within its precincts. We will form with you an alliance far more advantageous to you than the one which bound you to the Romans. Let not fear of Mahomet induce you to a step so adverse to your interests." All to whom the opportunity offered departed, notwithstanding these assurances. The rest, after deliberating upon the best course to be pursued, went with their magistrates and prostrated themselves at the feet of the sultan, presenting him the keys of the city. He received them with great kindness and addressed to them a few words calculated to inspire confidence. Only five large vessels set sail; the remainder were abandoned by the sailors. These, being favored by the wind, left the harbor of a city once so flourishing, whose destinies were so soon to change under the yoke of the infidel. The Venetian galleys followed the example of the Genoese and departed from the capital.

"O city, capital of all other cities!" exclaims the historian Ducas, whose grief at the sight of the condition of Constantinople finds vent in touching lamentations, "O city, centre of the world, the glory of Christians and the confusion of barbarians, O city, second paradise, planted with all trees fertile in spiritual fruit! Paradise, where is thy beauty? State, people, army, once so numerous, you have disappeared as a vessel which goes down at sea. Superb houses, magnificent palaces, sacred temples, I address you to-day as if you were living beings and could listen to my lamentations, and like Jeremiah, I call you to witness my sorrow and my tears. . . . What tongue is eloquent enough to depict the excess of misery and disgrace endured by the inhabitants when they were transported, not from Jerusalem to Babylon and Assyria, but from Constantinople to Syria, Egypt, Armenia, Persia, Arabia, Africa, Asia Minor and many other provinces, where their language was not spoken, and where their religion and their Sacred Writings were unknown? Sun, and you also, O earth, tremble and weep over the utter ruin of our nation, which God, by a just judgment, decreed in punishment of our sins."

Thus fell, under the sword of the Ottomans, the city seated on seven hills, the ancient Byzantium, eleven hundred and twenty-five years after its reconstruction by Constantine the Great. This destiny, for a long time presaged by the internal dissensions of the empire and the moral degredation of her sovereigns and people, was reserved by divine Providence for the House of the Palæologi, the first of the name having solicited against his country the protection and assistance of the Turkish prince. His weak successors, almost all of whom were either imprudent or cowardly, appeared as courtiers before the sultan, served as mercenaries in his armies, and conquered cities in his name. In gratitude for the assistance, so zealously tendered to the Ottoman arms, Mahomet destroyed the nationality of the people whom he subjugated.

CHAPTER IX.

MAHOMET AT CONSTANTINOPLE—CONQUEST OF PELOPONNESUS—END OF THE DYNASTY OF THE PALÆOLOGI.

Entry of Mahomet into Constantinople—Church of St. Sophia transformed into a mosque—Notaras conducted before Mahomet—The head of the Greek emperor exposed upon a column—Visit of the sultan to the grand duke—His entry into the imperial palace—Death of Lucas Notaras and his children—Departure of the fleet laden with booty—Election of a patriarch—Return of the sultan to Adrianople—Insurrection of the Greeks and the Albanian auxiliaries against Demetrius and Thomas, brothers of the emperor Constantine—Tourkhan dispatched to the aid of the Greek princes—His advice to Demetrius and Thomas—Submission of the Albanians—Dissensions between Demetrius and Thomas—Cruelty of Thomas—Success of Mahomet—The whole southern coast of Peloponnesus subjugated by the Ottomans—Thomas renews hostilities against the Turks and his brother—The sultan marches a second time against the two despots—Fate of Demetrius and Thomas Palæologus—End of the Greek rule in Peloponnesus—Fall of Trebizond—The empress Helen—Humiliation of the last Palæologi—Sorrow and terror of Europe—Useless efforts to excite a crusade.

MAHOMET did not wish to enter the city with the assailants; he waited outside the walls until he was informed that Constantinople was entirely in the hands of his troops. He made his triumphal entry through the gate of St. Romain into the capital of the empire he had destroyed. He was accompanied by his viziers, his pashas, his guards and a brilliant court; according to Ducas, each one of these was gifted with the strength of Hercules and the skill of Apollo, and on the field of battle was equal to ten other men. The conqueror was struck with astonishment and surprise on beholding the beautiful situation of the city, seated upon seven hills, and upon viewing its palaces and churches, their majestic domes gilded by the rays of the sun. On entering the hippodrome, his attention was attracted by a singular monument of antiquity, consisting of a brass column formed of the bodies of three serpents twined round each other. It had formerly supported the golden tripod consecrated in the temple of Delphi by the Greeks, in gratitude for their victory over Xexes. As an evidence of his strength, Mahomet broke with one stroke of his battle-axe the lower jaw of one of these monsters, which were regarded by the Turks as the idols or talismans of Constantinople.

Having arrived at the basilica of St. Sophia, he dismounted at the grand entrance and seemed eager to take possession of this superb cathedral of the Church of the East. He contemplated with delight and admiration its hundred and seven columns, covered with the rarest marbles and the granite of Thessaly, Epirus and Egypt; the eight porphyry columns, the pious offering of a Roman lady, removed from the Temple of the Sun constructed by Aurelian at Baalbec; the eight columns of green marble from the ancient temple of Diana at Ephesus, presented by the magistrates of that city; and other columns taken from temples consecrated to Jupiter at Cyzica, Athens and the Cyclades, and the pavement formed of marble brought from Thessaly and the country of the Molossians. The collosal statues of the apostles and of Christ, of the saints and angels, the large number of beautifully finished mosaics, and the ornaments of the altar, fixed the eye of Mahomet. He viewed with equal delight the galleries and arches. As he descended from the cupola, he perceived a soldier occupied in breaking some precious marble slabs, the veining of which so closely resembled waves, that from the four doors of the church the water seemed to be flowing out, emblematic of the four rivers of Paradise. Desirous of preserving this monument of his glory, he dealt the soldier a heavy blow with his cimeter, saying, "I gave you the treasures of the city and the prisoners, but the edifices belong to me."

Having completed the examination of the temple, the conqueror ordered a muezzin to call the people to prayer from the top of the loftiest tower; ascending the high altar, where a few days before the Christian mysteries had been celebrated, he himself consecrated the cathedral of St. Sophia to Islamism. The costly vessels and rich vestments which served for Christian worship had already been removed by the soldiers; it only remained to overthrow the cross. The walls, enriched with paintings in fresco and with mosaics were washed, purified, divested of every ornament by the infidels. The vaults of the temple erected in honor of the Word and of the Divine Wisdom, resounded henceforth to the Mussulman's cry: *There is but one God and Mahomet is his prophet.*

Erected by Constantine the Great, the church of St. Sophia had been twice burned during a disturbance by the mob, and it had been also injured by an earthquake. Theodosius the younger first, and

Justinian next, raised it from its ruins. Under the latter emperor, the architect, Anthemius of Tralles, drew up the plan and employed ten thousand workmen to execute it. Justinian himself daily superintended their labors and excited their activity by praises and rewards. At the solemn feast of the dedication, five years, eleven months and ten days after the first stone had been laid, he exclaimed with pious vanity: "I give thee glory, O God! who hast granted me to finish so great a work. O Solomon! I have surpassed you." This temple, which at the present moment is an imposing monument of the glorious reign of this prince, was the scene of magnificent court pomps and of the holy festivals of religion. It was used for coronations, triumphs, marriages of the emperors, the public ceremonies of the church, and for ecclesiastical assemblies and councils: it was the sanctuary not only of the capital, but of the whole empire, the master-piece of sacred architecture in Christendom.

It was the custom of the Greek emperors, after having gained a victory over their enemies, to terminate their triumphal march by a prayer in the basilica of St. Sophia. To conform to this custom, Mahomet assumed possession of the empire by his prayer at the high altar of this temple. But although the Turks preserved this majestic edifice, they did not spare the other churches, which Justinian and succeeding Greek emperors had erected in the most frequented quarters of Constantinople and its environs, on the shores of the sea and on the heights overlooking the coasts of Asia and Europe. They were sacked by the Turks, and the beautiful statuary broken to pieces.

Upon leaving the temple of Divine Wisdom, now transformed into a mosque, Mahomet ordered the admiral, Lucas Notaras, to be brought before him. "Contemplate," he said to him, "the heaps of the slain, the throng of captives; behold the result of your refusal to surrender the city." "My lord," replied Notaras, "it was not in my power nor in that of the emperor to deliver Constantinople to you, particularly after my master received letters urging him to resistance." The sultan's suspicions fell immediately upon Khalil-Pasha; but concealing his feelings, he enquired if the emperor had embarked on one of the Genoese vessels which had so fortunately escaped from the harbor. Notaras replied that he did not know, as he was at the palace when the Turks entered the city. At that moment the sultan received information that the emperor had been killed by two Janizaries. He ordered a search to be made for his body, and the head to be brought to him. He spoke kindly to Notaras, and directed a large sum of money to be given to him, his wife and each of his children; promising moreover to restore him his property and the offices he had held under the emperor. Flattered by these favors, the trator Notaras furnished the sultan a list of the principal officers of the court and of the State. Mahomet offered a reward for the heads of all of them.

The corpse of Constantine was found amid a heap of the slain. His head, with that of Orkhan, was laid at the feet of the conqueror. Constantine the Great dedicated to the memory of his mother, Helena, a square facing the church of St. Sophia, and named it Augusteon. In this square the emperor

Theodosius had erected a leaden column sermounted by a silver statue of himself, weighing fourteen thousand eight hundred marks (7,400 lbs.). Justinian I. replaced the leaden column by one of porphyry; and the silver statue of Theodosius made way for a colossal bronze statue representing Justinian on horseback, holding in his left hand a globe surmounted by a cross, and extending his right towards the east to represent his dominion over that portion of the world. On the summit of this column, under the feet of the horse of Justinian the victorious, was laid the head of the most courageous and most unfortunate of the Greek emperors: a cruel irony, when we remember the custom in the east of addressing a conqueror with thé words: "May the heads of thy enemies fall under thy horses' feet!" During the day this bloody trophy remained exposed to the public gaze; in the evening the skin was removed from the head and sent in sign of triumph to the princes of Persia, Arabia and many Turkish provinces. The Greeks were permitted to bury their emperor with funeral honors. Those who had escaped being made prisoners were allowed to remain at Galata. The last grand duke of the Byzantium empire, Notaras, continued to occupy his palace in the city.

The following day Mahomet traversed Constantinople on horseback and visited the grand duke in his palace. Notaras went out to meet him and placed all his treasures at his feet, saying they had been reserved for him. "Who then," demanded Mahomet angrily, "gave me possession of the city and all its treasures?" "God," answered the trembling Notaras. "Then," said the sultan, "my thanks are due to God and not to you." Harsh as seemed, he nevertheless visited the wife of Notaras, an aged princess, confined to bed by illness. He addressed her with tender expressions of filial respect. "I beg you, mother," he said to her, "not to be afflicted by what has happened; we must submit to the orders of God. I can return you more than you have lost. Let your only care be to recover your health." He sent for the sons of the grand duke, who threw themselves at his feet and humbly thanked him for his kindness. Mahomet continued his passage through the desolate city, which presented the appearance of a vast desert, meeting an occasional band of marauders in search of the booty which might have escaped the sack of the preceeding day.

Returning from his inspection of the capital, the sultan entered the imperial palace. Struck by the mournful solitude of these apartments, the dwelling of the hundred successors of Constantine, and once so brilliant, he quoted a Persian verse sadly applicable to its present condition: "The spider has spun its web in the palace of the Cæsars; the royal halls of Efrasiab resound to the mournful cry of the screech-owl." This philosophical reflection upon the instability of human grandeur, did not prevent Mahomet from abandoning himself to the intoxication of his triumph and to every gratification. A splendid banquet was prepared to which the sultan invited the most illustrious persons of his empire; he there drank to excess, and when nearly overpowered by wine, he ordered one of his officers to bring him Notaras' youngest son, a boy about fourteen years of age. The father, in despair, told the messenger of the tyrant that he would never willingly part with his son, that he would rather perish under the axe of the executioner. Indignant at the refusal, Mahomet sent an order to the executioner to bring before him Notaras, his sons, and Cantacuzenas, his son-in-law. Notaras bade adieu to his wife, and presented himself in the banquet hall. The sultan reserved the youngest to serve as his page, and ordered the others to be beheaded. At this last moment, the grand duke recovered the elevation of soul which had deserted him. As his children deplored their fate with cries and lamentations, the father consoled them, exhorting them to die as Christians, adding "Thou art just, O Lord!" When his sons had been executed in his presence, he asked the executioner to allow him to enter a few moments in a neighboring chapel to offer a prayer. The bodies of his children were still palpitating when he returned and was himself beheaded. The remains were cast into the street and remained unburied. The heads were carried to the tyrant who placed them before him upon his table. Other notable Spaniards, Venetians and Greek lords, whose lives had been spared at first, afterwards fell victims to the ferocity of the conqueror. A few saved their lives by paying seventy thousand ducats to Saganos Pasha.

Mahomet lost no time in completing the work of conquest, and the third day after the fall of the city he gave orders for the departure of the fleet, that he might with more tranquility meditate his vast designs. The vessels were heavily laden with precious stuffs, gold and silver, plate, brass, copper and bronze vases, a large number of books and prisoners of every condition. The tents of the camp were as full of booty as the ships. Dogs were led by chains of gold; the housings of horses were of gold cloth. Books were heaped in wagons and transported to the east and the west; ten volumes of Aristotle, of Plato, with works of theology were sold for one piece of money. Thus it happened that the noblest productions of the literature of the ancient Greeks were destroyed or dispersed. Fortunately, a portion of this classic wealth was securely placed in Italy, and the discovery made by German workmen now braves the ravages of time and barbarians. The Turks tore off the gold from the beautiful bindings of the Sacred Scriptures, sold the gold, and cast the books aside as useless. Pictures were burned and statues destroyed.

At last these scenes of devastation came to an end. The day after the departure of the fleet, Mahomet made his triumphal entrance into Constantinople, empty and desolate, without a monarch and without inhabitants; the city, however, could not be deprived of its admirable position, which will always fit it to be the capital of a great empire. In the midst of the public rejoicing, the sultan considered, as a true statesman, the manner of securing his conquest by such regulations as were suitable to the customs and wants of his subjects. By proclamation he invited all the inhabitants who had concealed themselves to return to their homes, where they should remain unmolested and be at liberty to live according to their former customs. To conciliate the affection of the Christians, the sultan respected their worship and discipline, and as their patriarch had just died, he desired them to elect a new spiritual chief, and to consecrate him with the usual ceremonies. Under the Christian emperors the newly elected patriarch was presented with a golden sceptre enriched with jewels, and a horse from the imperial stables magnificently caparisoned; mounted on this, the highest dignitary of the Church, accompanied by the body of the clergy, went to the palace of the patriarch, where the priests offered him their homage. The emperor, seated on his throne with uncovered head, handed him the crosier, the symbol of ecclesiastical authority. The hymns appropriated for the occasion having been sung, the emperor arose, holding the sceptre in his right hand; standing on his right was the Cæsar, on his left the metropolitan of Heraclea. The patriarch thrice saluted the assembly, and prostrated himself at the feet of the emperor. The monarch, elevating his sceptre, pronounced aloud the following words: "The Holy Trinity, Who has bestowed the empire upon me, confers upon you the patriarchate of the new Rome."

As soon as the Senator George Scholarius, also known under the name of Gennadius, had been elected by the small number of ecclesiastics remaining, Mahomet required that the usual ceremonies should be observed. The patriarch was conducted by the electors to the grand hall of the imperial palace, which was magnificently adorned. The sultan, having invested him with his new dignity, gave him a splendid repast, conversing with him in the most cordial manner; he made him a present of a jeweled sceptre, emblem of the civil and religious authority conferred upon him saying: "May heaven protect you! Under all circumstances, rely upon my friendship and enjoy all the privileges possessed by your predecessors." Mahomet then accompanied him to the very gate of the palace and presented him a white horse richly caparisoned. He ordered the viziers and pashas to conduct him to his residence.

Having established good order in Constantinople, Mahomet turned his attention to the Genoese of Galata. He ordered the census to be taken of those who remained in the city. The houses of those who had escaped were forced open, but were preserved from pillage. An inventory was made of the furniture, and a delay of three months was granted during which the proprietors could return. But this term having expired, the property was to be confiscated. The sultan ordered the soldiers to demolish the walls of Galata on the side of the land, but he left untouched that portion of the enclosure resting on the harbor. He collected a large number of masons and workmen to repair the injury done by the Turkish artillery, and also to add to the fortifications of Constantinople, which he made the metropolis of the Ottoman empire to the prejudice of Bursa and Adrianople, which became provincial cities. He directed also, under penalty of death, that five thousand families from Anatolia and Roumaina, should come, and occupy the vacant houses in the capital before the end of September.

By public proclamations, he promised that all Greeks, who could prove their noble birth, should be treated with more distinction than they had enjoyed under the emperor. Many nobles relying upon these promises repaired to Constantinople upon the appointed day, but they paid for their blind confidence with their lives.

Twenty days after the fall of Constantinope, Mahomet set out for Adrianople, carrying with him an immense booty and a large number of slaves, among whom were many noble Greek ladies and young girls. The wife of the grand-duke Notaras, an intrepid and virtuous woman, much beloved by the poor for her extreme charity, died on the way. The sultan also conducted as a prisoner his grand vizier Khalil, who had been bought by the gold of the Greeks. After forty days of captivity, he was beheaded and his friends were forbidden to weep for his death. From Adrianople, which he entered with triumphal pomp, Mahomet addressed messages to the Sultan of Egypt, the Shah of Persia, and the Scherif of Mecca, announcing the conquest of Constantinople. Adrianople soon witnessed the arrival of numbers of Christian princes or their ambassadors who went to congratulate the sultan and offer him presents. The conqueror, seated on a lofty throne, received them with arrogance and summoned them to pay their annual tribute.

We must now trace the history of the last dynasty which reigned at Constantinople to its extinction. Demetrus and Thomas Palæologus, brothers of Constantine and despots of Morea, were overwhelmed with consternation at the news of the death of the emperor and the destruction of the Greek monarchy. Having no hope of being able to resist the formidable enemies of the Greeks, they determined to establish themselves in Italy, with a few nobles, who were willing to follow their fortunes. Mahomet relieved their anxiety by exacting of them only the payment of an annual tribute of twelve thousand ducats. But the respite of seven years which he granted Morea, whilst he ravaged the continent and islands, was a period of suffering, discord, and misery. In place of Constantine, the archons wished to proclaim Demetrius, the elder of the surviving brothers; Thomas, the younger, who was ambitious and tyrannical, was unwilling to yield the crown, and the two divided Peloponnesus. Dissensions next broke out among the Greeks, and Emmanuel Cantacuzenus, aiming at the supreme authority, headed a faction which repulsed the Palæologi. On the other hand, the Albanian auxiliaries refused obedience to the two despots, ravaged the country, and offered the Turks to pay the same amount of tribute as the Greeks with the view of thus securing the sovereignty of Peloponnesus.

Next to Emmanuel Cantacuzenus, the two most dangerous chiefs of the revolt against Demetrius and Thomas were two Greeks, Kenterion Zacharias and Lukanos, brothers-in-law of the emperor Constantine, whom Thomas had, for some time, held as prisoners. These two captives succeeded in making their escape, and joined by the Albanians and the Greek rebels, they threatened to deprive the Palæologi of the government of Peloponnesus which had been accorded them by the sultan. The rule of these princes would have been brought to an end, had not Hasan, the Greek commander at Corinth, solicited aid from the Porte. Tourakham, who thirty years before, had pushed his conquests as far as Lacedenon, was sent with his sons and a Turkish army to Peloponnesus to protect the Greeks against the Albanians (1454). He assembled the Palæologi, and exhorted them to act in concert with the Greeks, who naturally would have more confidence in them, their countrymen, than in him, their former enemy, although now their ally.

"If the sultan," he said in conclusion, "had not taken pity on you and aided you to maintain possession of your thrones, which were almost lost to you, you would now be wanderers and exiles. You must admit that your administration has been very bad; there exists then for you an absolute necessity to govern your subjects with more wisdom. I particularly exhort you not to hasten your destruction by your domestic dissensions. Put down with a strong hand any attempt to rebel, Chastise without mercy the wicked and reward the good. The proper distribution of punishments and recompenses has elevated the Turks to the summit of power."

Tourakhan, having thus advised the two brothers, marched against the Albanians. The despot Demetrius, at the head of a small body of Greeks, followed the Turks to the defiles of Barbostenis, where the Albanians had placed the women and children for protection. The Turks and the Greeks united their efforts against the enemy. In the night the Albanians took flight, and ten thousand women fell into the hands of the Turks. Thomas, with another division of the army, marched towards the city of Œtos, which had declared in favor of Kenterion; it purchased peace by the surrender of a thousand slaves, arms, and provisions. Tourakhan obtained the prompt submission of the other Albanian chiefs by allowing them to keep the horses they had taken from the Greeks.

Before his departure, Mahomet's lieutenant again exhorted Demetrius and Thomas to live in peace with each other. "If you are united," he said, "you will prosper; but if you are at variance, your undertakings will not succeed. Make yourselves respected by your subjects and punish crime inexorably." Far from profiting by the wise counsels of Tourkhoman, the Greek princes displayed no vigor and were even more indulgent to their subjects, hoping thus to secure their fidelity, whilst in reality they were encouraging conspiracies and a spirit of innovation. The chief rebel, Lukanos, united a few of the Byzantines, the Albanians and Peloponnesians in a conspiracy, having for its aim to render the cities independent of their despot. The conspirators applied to the commander Hasan, who rejected their proposition to refer the matter to the Porte, as they were unable to pay the tribute which had been imposed. Besides, Demetrius and Thomas baffled their projects by sending to the court of Istambal their annual tribute of twelve thousand ducats. Pleased with this promptitude, the sultan expedited a decree addressed to the principal families of Peloponnesus, in which he swore by the great prophet Mahomet, by the seven Korans, by the hundred and twenty-four prophets, by his own sabre, by the soul of his father, that he would suffer no injury to be done to them, their children, nor their possessions; that they should live in peace and should be better protected than under the reign of his predecessors.

But with an inexplicable disregard of the dangers to which they were exposed, the two despots soon weakened their power by domestic quarrels, which were appeased neither by the ties of relationship, the oaths exchanged at the foot of the altar, nor the imperious force of necessity. Spandurgino says, so great was the hatred between the two brothers, that one would have eaten the heart of the other. Always fighting to satisfy their hatred, they consumed in an unnatural war, the alms and resources sent from the west, and used their power only to inflict barbarous and arbitrary punishments. Thomas, who was no less tyrannical than the sultan, although far inferior to him in ability and power, reproduced in Peloponnesus the scenes of violent usurpation and the assassinations so often repeated by Mahomet. In order to obtain possession of Glarenza and Achaïa, he enticed the lord of these districts, his relative, to Patras, under the pledge of a safe conduct. Then he cast him, with his sons, into prison, where they died of starvation. He exercised atrocious cruelties on the son-in-law of the prince of Achaïa; he cut off his hands, nose and ears and plucked out his eyes. In his insatiable ambition, he despoiled of his possessions and deprived of sight Theodore Bokali, one of the great proprietors of Peloponnesus. Emmanuel Cautacuzenus, for whom he intended the same fate, succeeded in escaping and placed himself at the head of the revolted Albanians. To please them he changed his Greek for an Albanian name, ravaged the low country and besieged the two despots, Thomas and Demetrius, in their residences of Patras and Sparta.

Mahomet had long meditated striking a final blow at the expiring power of these two princes. He considered the general disorder to be favorable to his designs of conquest. On the 5th of May, 1458, he set out from Constantinople with a large force, leaving on the way a division to besiege Corinth, and proceeded as far as Phlius in Peloponnesus, whose Albanian commander, Doxias, determined to offer a vigorous resistance, and retired with the inhabitants and his troops to a fortified eminence, whence he could defend the approach to the city. The sultan despising so weak an enemy, marched upon Harsos, whose garrison surrendered on the first demand. The Albanians who had sought refuge at Harsos attempted to escape, and Mahomet resolved to make an example of them to prevent others from imitating them. By his order, the ankle and wrist bones of twenty of these unfortunate fugitives were broken by blows of large clubs, and they were left thus mutilated to die in slow torture. The place of this atrocious execution received the Turkish name of Tokmak-Hissari (castle of bones). Another city, Ætos, situated on a mountain, was reduced to such extremity by the want of water, that the inhabitants moistened their bread with the blood of the beasts of burden, which they slaughtered. Overpowered by their sufferings, they were on the point of capitulating, when the Janizaries scaled the ramparts and pillaged the city. Mahomet next led his army to the city of Rupela, also called Akoba, where the Albanians and Greeks had sought an asylum with their families. After two days of combat, many of his soldiers were disabled, and he was about to withdraw his troops, when a deputation arrived in his camp offering to capitulate the city. It was spared, but the inhabitants were transferred to Constantinople. Having reached Pazenica, the sultan, through Cantacuzenus, summoned the Albanian garrison to surrender, but the proposition was rejected, and they resisted the Ottoman troops. Cantacuzenus, being suspected of encouraging them in their defence, lost the favor of Mahomet. In two days the sultan passed on to Tagea, where he was undecided whether to march upon Sparta, the asylum of the despot Thomas, or upon Epidaurus, then the residence of Demetrius. Finding the route from Tegea impossible for an army, he returned to invest Moklia or Moukhla. This place, defended by Asanes Demetrius, was advantageously situated upon an inaccessible mountain, After uselessly attempting to negotiate, Mahomet directed his batteries against the city, and destroyed the outer rampart. The brave defenders retired behind their second line of fortifications, and resisted most obstinately. But the enemy having managed to come to an understanding with some parties within the walls, Asanes Demetrius and Lukanos of Sparta, decided to surrender. "Say to your master," the sultan answered the envoys sent by them, "that I am ready to grant him peace and my friendship, upon condition that the portion of Peloponnesus now occupied by my troops shall be mine, that he will pay an annual tribute of five hundred pounds of gold for the part which he still possesses; as to Thomas, the prince of Patras, tell him that unless he cede his principality to me, I will take it from him by force of arms." Asanes Demetrius and Lukanos carried this message to the two despots. The uninterrupted success of the Ottoman arms decided the despots to accept the conditions imposed by the conqueror (July 4, 1458). Thus all the southern coast of Peloponnesus passed into the hands of the Ottomans.

Before his departure for Constantinople, Mahomet visited Athens, of which Tourakhan had just taken possession. From that place he sent a messenger to the despots of Peloponnesus, demanding the ratification of the treaty, and the hand of the daughter of Demetrius in marriage. The despots signed the treaty, and Demetrius, following the disgraceful example of some of his ancestors, gave his daughter to Mahomet. Thomas soon violated his oath. Yielding to the suggestions of Lukanos Nicephoras, he raised the standard of revolt, took Calaveita from the Ottomans, and a number of cities from Demetrius, who immediately collected his forces and invested Scutari and Akoba.

Mahomet, attributing the insurrection to the negligence of the son of Tourakhan, deprived him of the government of Morea, and conferred it upon Hamsa. He forced the Greeks to raise the siege of Patras, and presented himself, with the despot, Demetrius, before Leontari, whither Thomas had retired. Thomas was defeated with a loss of two hundred men. The Ottomans continued to devastate the country, until the two brothers, seeing their ruin inevitable, met at Karritza, and were apparently reconciled.

Mahomet threw the blame of this alliance upon Hamsa, and replaced him in his command by Seganos-Pasha. When he arrived, he found the two brothers again in open hostility. Thomas had violated his oath, had taken possession of Laconia and Messina, his brother's domains, and he was besieging Kalamata. He entered into negotiations with the sultan, who was willing to accept the offers of Thomas upon certain conditions. Far from keeping his promises, the despot was unable to fulfil even the stipulations of the former treaty. The moment of vengeance had, at last, arrived. Mahomet marched in person against the two brothers, (April, 1460,) and soon appeared before Sparta. In his distress, Demetrius sought to shelter himself against the perfidy of his brother by betraying the cause of Greece. He had recourse to their common master; he repaired to the camp of the sultan, who received him with extreme kindness, promised him anew to marry his daughter and to indemnify him for the cession of his turbulent province. Mahomet retained Demetrius near his person, placed a Turkish garrison in Sparta, took and pillaged Kastriza. He did not pardon the garrison for their valiant resistance which had cost the loss of many of his Janizaries. Notwithstanding the voluntary submission of these warriors, three hundred were conducted to the public square and massacred; the commander was sawn in two. The sultan next directed his march to Leontari. The city was taken by assault, and six thousand slain, men and women, heaped indiscriminately with the bodies of beasts of burden attested the victory and vengeance of Mahomet, who forbade the men to spare the life even of a slave. He promised the garrison a free pardon when it capitulated; he swore that none of its defenders should be slain, nor reduced to slavery, nor even injured in any manner. But as soon as they came out from the fortifications, he assembled all, woman as well as men, to the number of thirteen hundred and massacred them without mercy. These atrocities spread terror throughout Peloponnesus, and the garrisons of nearly all the other fortresses sent deputies to offer their submission. Crocontelos, the commander of St. George, cast himself at the feet of the sultan. Navarin and Arkadia, the two most strongly fortified ports of the Western coast, surrendered without attempting a defence. Ten thousand inhabitants of the latter place were transported to Constantinople to people the suburbs of the city. The despot Demetrius, brother of the magnanimous Constantine Dragoses, followed in the suite of the victor and witnessed the cruelties exercised upon the Greeks. According to the suggestion of this prince, who was unworthy of the blood which flowed in his veins, Mahomet dispatched Isa, grandson of Ewrenos, towards the Eastern coast of Morea, to take possession of Napoli of Malvoisia, and to bring back the wife and daughter of the despot. Nicholas Palæologus refused to give up the city; but he allowed the princess and his daughter to depart with Isa; the sultan sent them to Bœotia and ordered Demetrius to join them there. The despot Thomas, losing all hope of success after the fall of Leontari, abandoned Kalamata and embarked with his children.

Confiding to the beglerbeg Saganos, the conquest of the remaining cities, Mahomet advanced along the coast to reconnoitre the Venetian ports of Modon and Pylos. The Venetians renewed their protestations of friendship to the sultan. The Turkish cavalry, nevertheless, continued their ravages around Pylos, carrying the Albanians captive. Mahomet returned to the north, taking possession on the way of a large number of cities which had not yet been subdued. The Albanian Doxas, the brave commander of Calaveita, was sawn in two. The Turks beheaded or sold as slaves the soldiers of the garrison. The city of Caritena, defended by the Palæologus Syceromalo, made a vigorous but ineffectual resistence. The castle of Salmenikos, under the command of another Palæologus, Graitzas, held out still longer against the enemy, after the city itself had been taken and pillaged. Graitzas offered to yield the palace to the sultan, upon condition that he would withdraw some distance from the city and not disturb the garrison during their retreat. Mahomet retired altogether leaving the affair in the hands of Hamsa who had been restored to his dignity of governor in the place of Saganos.

Returning to Peloponnesus, the sultan passed through Athens, where he received information that Franco Acciainoli, his former favorite, was conspiring to achieve his independence. He conducted ten of the principal citizens as hostages to Constantinople, and ordered Saganos to get rid of Franco. Saganos executed the order faithfully, and the last duke of Athens was strangled in his own tent. By his death the whole of Greece, with the exception of a few ports belonging to the Venetians, fell into the hands of the Ottomans. Mahomet assigned the city of Ainos as the residence of the despot Demetrius, and appointed him an annual revenue for his support, but his daughter was not deemed worthy to become the wife of the sultan. The despot, Thomas, took refuge in Europe. His misfortunes obtained for him the hospitality of the Vatican; the pope and cardinals granted him a pension of six thousand ducats. Thus in the tenth year of his reign and the seventh after the fall of Constantinople, Mahomet had utterly destroyed the government of the Greeks in Peloponnesus, and subjugated the whole of Greece with the exception of Coron, Modon, Pylos, Monembasia and Naupacta; he had taken captive, expelled, strangled the princes of Laconia, Achaia and Attica, burned, depopulated their cities, subjected their defenders to the most cruel tortures. Therefore hatred of the Turks became rooted and hereditary in the hearts of the Greek people, who for more than three hundred years fought with indefatigable energy to recover the independence they had lost by their own dissensions.

The following year the despot Demetrius was joined in his exile by a companion in misfortune, David, the last of the princely race of Commenes, who, after the taking of Constantinople by the Latins, had laid the foundation of a new empire on the coast of the Black Sea. The sultan, pursuing his conquests in Asia Minor, attacked by sea and land the capitol of David, who had assumed the empty title of emperor of Trebizond. Appearing before this city, from which his admiral had been repulsed with considerable loss, he sent an envoy to David, with orders to address him peremptorily: "Will you preserve your life and wealth by resigning your crown, or do you prefer to lose your crown, your wealth, and your life?" The weak David followed the example of the neighboring Mussulman, Prince of Sinope, who had delivered to the imperious Ottoman a fortified city, his artillery and garrison. He surrendered Trebizond and his kingdom to Mahomet, who assigned him the city of Seres for his residence and a revenue nearly equal to that which he sacrificed. The articles of capitulation were faithfully executed, and after the ratification the deposed monarch embarked with his family for Constantinople. The Turks took immediate possession of Trebizond; the young men were distributed among the Spahis and Janizaries, the wealthiest citizens were sent to the capital, and the remainder of the population were removed to the suburbs. Mahomet retained in captivity the nephew of David, son of his brother and predecessor John, the legitimate heir of the throne usurped by David. The youngest of the eight sons of this unfortunate prince, renouncing the faith of his fathers, embraced Islamism at Adrianople. In this ancient abode of the Cæsars, the last two princes of the Byzantine empire met at the gate of the sultan, the Palæologus, Demetrius, and the Commenes David, both driven from their kingdoms, both living through the pity of their haughty conqueror, and kissing the dust under his feet.

Not content with destroying the empire of Trebizond, Mahomet resolved to exterminate the family of Comnenes. Suspected for some frivolous cause of keeping up a correspondence with the king of Persia, Ouzoun-Hasan, the husband of his niece, David, with all his family, was cast into prison at Adrianople. The sultan, returning from Constantinople, ordered David to be brought before him, and gave him his choice between the Koran or death. The prince refused to abjure his religion, and his implacable enemy pronounced the decree of death against the entire family, ordering the bodies to be left without burial to serve as food for the dogs and birds of prey. The sentence was executed at Constantinople: David, his brother Alexias, his nephew, the younger son of his brother John, and seven of his own sons fell under the axe of the executioner. The eighth was spared because he was a Mussulman. The daughter of David, whom the sultan had rejected as his wife, afterwards married Saganos, the governor of Thessaly, stipulating that she should preserve her religion; but in order to contract later a second marriage with a son of Ewrenos, she did not hesitate to embrace Islamism. The empress Helen suffered courageously and, like the mother of the Maccabees, died gloriously. In contempt of the sentence of the tyrant, whose anger she alone dared to brave, she rendered the last duties to her husband and sons. Clad in a coarse linen garment, she repaired to the place of execution, dug a grave with her own hands, watched by the remains during the day to drive away the dogs and birds of prey, and at night confided to the earth the dear objects of her tenderness, cruelly immolated to the cupidity of the tyrant. The faithful wife and pious mother, overwhelmed by grief, did not long survive her loss.

The unfortunate Demetrius, whose abject submission excited the pity and contempt of Mahomet, survived the family of Comnenes. At last he assumed the monks gown to bury all remembrance of the imperial mantle. The self-imposed exile of the despot Thomas, was, perhaps, as humiliating as the servitude of his brother. He left two sons, Andrew and Manuel, who were educated in Italy. The elder, despised by his enemies and a disgrace to his friends, degraded himself by his conduct and marriage. He sold successively to the kings of France and Aragon, his title of heir to the empires of Constantinople and Trebizond. Manuel Palæologus wished to revisit his native land. His return could cause no anxiety at the Porte, and the Sultan assigned him considerable revenues. When he died, his funeral obsequies were honored by a large concourse of Mussulmans and Christians. He left one son undistinguished amid the crowd of Turkish slaves, whose dress, manners and religion he was not ashamed to adopt. Thus fell, in the west and the east, the imperial race of Byzantium, crushed by shame and drowned in blood; thus the Greek power in Europe and Asia was concentrated in himself, by the lord of the two seas and the two quarters of the world, as Mahomet II. styled himself after the fall of Constantinople.

After the Turks became masters of Constantinople, Europe comprehened the magnitude of the loss which was destined to be the cause of a long series of wars and calamities to the nations which lay near the Ottoman domains. In future, their armies could invade Hungary unimpeded; Hungary once subjugated, Italy and the empire of Germany were exposed to attack. The Russians deeply regretted not having sent aid to Greece, which had long been for them a second country. The Russians remembered with gratitude that to Greece they owed Christianity, a knowledge of the arts, and different advantages of social life. In the city of Moscow, people then regarded Constantinople, as in modern Europe, Paris was regarded under the reign of the greatest King of France, Louis XIV. They had no other model for the magnificence of church ceremonies, for courtly pomp, for matters of taste and opinions. And yet, whilst deploring the fate of Constantinople, wearing the yoke of the foreigner, whilst compassionating the miseries of the Greeks, their historians rendered an impartial verdict of them and the Turks. Without fear of the laws, an empire is an unbridled courser. Constantine and his ancestors permitted the nobles to oppress the people; justice was no longer found in their tribunals, nor courage in their hearts; the judges gathered their wealth from the tears and blood of the innocent; the Greek soldier was proud only of the beauty of his garments; the citizen did not blush to advance his interests by perfidy; the soldier was not ashamed to fly. God at last hurled his thunder bolts against unworthy sovereigns, by raising up Mahomet, whose warriors sport with death on the battle field, and whose judges are incorruptible. Thus have been accomplished the predictions of St. Methodius and St. Leo the Wise, who long ago foretold that the sons of Ismael should conquer Byzantium; perhaps we may also see accomplished the remainder of the prophecy, which promises the Russians a triumph over the children of Ismael and the sovereignty of the seven hills of Constantinople.

Sorrow and terror enkindled among other nations of Europe the enthusiasm of the crusades. In the first moments of surprise, Philip the Good, Duke of Burgundy, a wise and aged prince offered to engage with all his forces in a crusade against the Ottomans. The principal knights and barons of his state imitated his example. But various circumstances caused the failure of the enterprise. Had a spark of this enthusiasm inflamed all hearts, had the union among Christian princes equalled their courage, had all the powers from Sweden to Naples risen against the infidels, the Europeans would undoubtedly have retaken Constantinople, and driven back the Turks to their former possessions. But the condition of the Christian world and the dispositions of the different rulers prevented the execution of such a project. "Each country," says Æneas Sylvius Piccolomini, who was familiar with the policy of this period, "is governed by a particular sovereign, and each prince is influenced by individual interests. What eloquence could collect under the same standard so great a number of powers, naturally discordant and hostile to each other? Even could their troops be united, who would dare to fill the office of general? What order could be established in such an army? What would be its discipline? Who would undertake to obtain supplies for so numerous a multitude? Who would understand their language, or who could bring under subjection to one rule men so different in customs? Who could reconcile the English and the French, the Genoese and Aragonese, the Germans and the people of Hungary and Bohemia? If this war be undertaken with a small body of troops, they will be overpowered by the infidels; if a large number be sent, they will be destroyed by their own disorders."

Some years later, this same Æneas Sylvius, having become pope under the name of Pius II. sounded the alarm against the Turks, and passed the remainer of his life in efforts to excite a crusade. At the council of Mantua were present deputies from Peloponnesus, Rhodes, Cyprus, Lesbos, Epirus, Illyria and from nearly all the sovereigns of Europe, and he endeavored to awaken in their hearts the zeal which animated his own. The assembly agreed to divide among the nations of Europe the expense of the war. For three years, they were to collect a tax of one-tenth of the revenue of the clergy, a thirtieth of the income of the laity, and a twentieth of the funds of the Jews destined to maintain fifty thousand men at arms. But discords and revolutions frustrated this design, and when the feeble and aged pontiff went to Ancona to place himself at the head of the crusade, he found there a multitude without commanders, without money or arms. All had some excuse for not fulfilling the engagement; the day of departure was indefinitely postponed, and the venerable head of the Church died suddenly at Ancona. The princes of Italy and the rest of Europe gave no further thought to the future, and renounced the project of a crusade. Ruled by momentary interests, they directed their efforts to their personal aggrandizement, without troubling themselves to oppose a barrier to the progress of a people, whose final triumph had been prepared by a long series of successes. They saw with indifference the Eastern gate of Europe in the hands of the infidels, and the foundation made by the Ottoman upon the ruins of the Greek power of a vast empire, which seemed to bid defiance to the Christian world.

FINIS.

www.ingramcontent.com/pod-product-compliance
Lightning Source LLC
Chambersburg PA
CBHW032205230426
43672CB00011B/2513